This book is dedicated to the pilots, crew, and pararescuemen of the 176th Airwing 210th and 212th Rescue Squadrons of the Alaska Air National Guard. Without their bravery and dedication to downed airmen, this book could have had a completely different ending.

Acknowledgments

This book would not have been possible without the encouragement of so many people. Several years ago, I started sharing our Alaskan experiences on Facebook. My friends and family enjoyed hearing about all of the predicaments that Shon and I were facing out in the bush and encouraged me to share more. I consistently heard that people were living in Alaska vicariously through us and wanted to hear about our day-to-day lives. After a while, these people in my life—many of whom I hadn't seen in thirty years or more—suggested that I write a book. After hearing that thought repeatedly, the idea was born. I toyed with it for quite some time while enjoying the connection with people online through my tales of our adventures and misadventures. The book idea would have remained a dream without a challenge from my adventurous husband. One day, as Shon and I were talking, I mentioned writing "the book" once again. Shon shocked me when he said, "Are you going to continue to talk about this book or actually write it?" At that moment, I knew I needed to get it done.

In less than an hour, I had an outline written. I called the only writer I knew, Tera Evans, and told her my idea. She was excited about the prospect and vowed to hold me to it. Another friend, Wendy Scott, was my first reader. I sent her the first several chapters and held my breath. She called me the next day, asking for the rest of the book. When I told her that it wasn't written yet, she informed me that I needed to get busy. She and her family wanted more. With all of that encouragement, I posted on Facebook that I was going for it. I requested suggestions from the people who had been reading my stories for years. I was overwhelmed with the response. To all of my friends and family who encouraged me, I want you to know that this would not have happened without your sweet words.

As the process got into full swing, more people became involved. My conscientious sister-in-law, Kandis Dobbs, was my first editor. Reading each word, she gently suggested ways to improve sentences so I "wouldn't make English teachers cringe." I also was introduced to another writer, Sara King, by her grandfather and my racquetball partner, Tom Brion. Tom had written a book with his granddaughter's help called *Stories I've Heard, Characters I've Met & Lies We've Told in My 44 Alaskan Years.* Sara helped me through the process of self-publishing. Without her valuable expertise, I am not sure this book would have made it to completion. At her suggestion, I sent the book to forty unbiased readers to get their feedback. I quickly dubbed them my fabulous forty. Their questions and suggestions showed me how to bring the book up a notch. Their work was invaluable. And my dear friend, Tera Evans, was my final editor.

To the people involved in the process and the people who are in the stories, I thank you. You have made this book what it is.

Table of Contents

List of Characters

Ann Parker – That's me

Shon Parker – my adventurous husband

Kyle and Jared – our two boys

Mirai – Kyle's wife

Walt – our air taxi pilot out of Willow

Roger – our neighbor across Cub Lake

Lilly, Peanut, and Chachi – Roger's dogs

Larry and Jody – freighters who barged our belongings up the Yentna River

Lucille Heater – Larry's wife and author of the book, *Life on the Yentna*

Ken Lee – snow machine freighter and Iron Dogger

Kuma – our precious German Shepherd

Cindi – owner of Skwentna Roadhouse

Bob and Ruth – original owners/builders of the cabin on Cub Lake

Steve – postmaster of the Skwentna Post Office

Bonnie – Steve's wife

Tom Brion – my racquetball partner and owner of Bentalit Lodge, author of the book *Stories I've Heard, Characters I've Met & Lies We've Told in My 44 Alaskan Years*

Patty – Tom's sweet wife and owner of Bentalit Lodge

Fishing Joe – our talkative friend

Jack – our friend who crashed his plane off of the end of our runway

Ray and Riska – friends with the Husky who called for help after Shon's crash

Johnny – original owner of N3227M

Mike – flight instructor

Kay – my seventh-grade English teacher I discovered in Alaska

Robert – Kay's husband and our airplane mechanic

FBI Billy – Johnny's neighbor who graciously offered us the use of his home

Russell – our first grandson

* Some names may have been changed for privacy.

Our Beginning

I can't say that it was love at first sight, but it was pretty dang close. I met Shon at Casino Night at Angelo State University in 1988 when I was a sophomore and he was a junior. He was hobbling around on crutches with a broken ankle. One leg of his jeans was cut so it would fit over the cast. I happened to notice tire tread marks along the leg with the cut. He was telling a group of friends that he had run over his ankle with a three-wheeler a couple of days before and seemed somewhat proud of the tire marks. I piped up and said, "So … don't you ever wash your pants?" I got a good laugh from the group, but Shon gave me a look that said, "Who do you think you are?" If I'd only known then that I'd be washing his pants for the rest of my life, I might not have been so glib.

Several months later, a mutual friend called me to ask if I would go with Shon to help him pick out a suit for a job interview. He was applying for the San Angelo Police Department as a police officer. My friend, Terri, had tried, but she hated shopping and hadn't been able to help. I readily agreed. I remembered the guy with the dirty pants. He was cute. We agreed on a time, and Shon came to pick me up at my apartment. We spent the entire day looking for an appropriate suit. I finally decided he wasn't suit material, so I suggested we go to a Western wear store. After a quick look around, I picked out a white shirt, brown jeans, and a sharp-looking Western jacket. His cowboy boots completed the outfit. When he stepped out of the dressing room, I'm pretty sure he saw on my face that we had found the perfect clothes for the interview. He looked good, really good. He was tall, fit, and easy on the eyes. I told myself to quit staring.

Even though we had had an enjoyable day shopping, I didn't hear from Shon for a while. I was bored one night and called Terri to see if she wanted to go to dollar night at the movies. On Tuesday nights, we could get in one of the local movie theaters for a buck each with our college IDs. She said she was studying for a final, but that I should call Shon or his roommate, Jeff. I thought about it for a bit. I'd met both of them and decided I would ask whichever one picked up the phone. As chance would have it, Shon answered and agreed to go with me to the movies. We had a wonderful time, laughing and talking. We enjoyed getting to know each other better that evening and the next several evenings. When Terri called me that Friday, she was shocked to find out that Shon and I were engaged. We got married five months later while he was in the police academy. Neither of us was impetuous, but we both knew right away that we were right for each other.

The happy-go-lucky man that I married slowly disappeared under the stress of his new career. Police work was strange. The hours were horrible. The days off were ridiculous. The stress was extreme.

2

Shon and Ann's Wedding Day, 1989
For more stories, photos, and videos, go to www.followmetoalaska.com.

The excitement was addictive. The camaraderie was unique. The temptations were real. And the degradation that Shon witnessed was gut-wrenching. Police work changes people.

While on patrol as a beat cop, Shon's eyes were opened to the evils of this world, including suicides and murders. He was spit on, cussed at, and threatened. As a child abuse investigator early in his career, his view of society took an even bigger hit. He investigated, in great detail, cases where children were severely physically abused. Other cases involved young children who were sexually assaulted by the very people who were supposed to love and protect them. While on the SWAT team, he raided drug houses and dealt with hostage situations. Later, as a highway patrolman, he saw the mangled bodies of people in car accidents while working the roads of his hometown, the very highways that his family traveled every day.

By the time Shon and I had two kids and had been married for eighteen years, we had both become cynical. He had worked as a city cop for half that time and as a state highway patrolman the other half. I stayed home with our kids for several years. When they were both old enough to start school, I returned to my teaching career. I loved teaching, but it, too, was extremely demanding. I taught algebra and geometry, but I dealt with teen pregnancies and students who were abusing drugs. I recognized the signs among students who were anorexic and those who were cutting themselves.

Shon saw the adults committing the atrocities. I saw the innocent victims in the faces of many of my students, several of whom were heading down the same dark path as their parents. The excitement for life and the hope of a wonderful future that we once had was now fading. Instead of expecting the best in life, we braced ourselves for the worst.

Life had kicked us in the teeth, and we needed a change. It came one evening when our son, Kyle, was getting his aviation badge for Scouts. We arranged a night flight with a friend. I hopped into the front seat of the little plane while Kyle and his brother, Jared, settled into the backseat. Shon sat in the truck on the taxiway watching as we took a short flight. After a few minutes, we landed, and Shon and I exchanged places. As I sat in the dark truck waiting for them to return, God presented me with an idea. Shon and I needed to get our pilots' licenses. That night after I put the kids to bed, I brought up the subject. I had carefully crafted my case, but I didn't need to worry. Shon was all in. He made all of the arrangements for us to get started the next day.

Over the next few months, I caught glimpses of the sweet man I had married. He was getting his spark back with this new, exciting endeavor. On September 10, 2006, I earned my pilot's license. Shon got his the next day. I like to point out that I was the first pilot in our family! It was less than a year later when a grand opportunity came along. Shon was so tired of the highway patrol, but he had a wife and two kids to support. Even though he felt stuck, God had provided a way out. The Texas Department of Public Safety posted ten openings for the Aircraft Division. Never before had they opened up so many opportunities at one time. With Shon's private pilot's license and his experience, he met the qualifications to apply. It was no surprise to me when he was promoted and headed to Austin for further training.

Shon had a blast flying, but he was still a police officer. Over the next ten years, he continued to see the evil in the world. Shon intercepted drugs, was involved in an extended gun battle from the air, dealt with severe border issues, and witnessed human trafficking. While in El Paso, he watched from above as bad guys sold drugs, guns, and hand grenades in public parking lots, places where we shopped! Even though Shon wasn't a beat cop anymore, he still found himself a witness to the worst in our society. Shon enjoyed his work because he was flying helicopters and airplanes, but the hours he put in increased as he promoted. The stress never decreased. It, too, only grew. Our time together was never sacred, so I often found myself alone after the boys grew up and moved away. By the time Shon was eligible for retirement after twenty-eight years in law enforcement, we both knew that it was time to leave police work. The stress of it was killing us both.

Early on in Shon's flying career, he heard about the flying opportunities that were available in our most northern state. When he first mentioned his interest in Alaska, I was shocked. Shon was the coldest-natured person I knew. His family told stories of Shon standing so close to the fire when he was a kid that they could smell his hair

5

*Shon making an interesting landing in the AStar
near Texas/Mexico border, 2011*

burning. People gave him a hard time for wearing a coat when it was seventy degrees outside. Our friends called him Lizard Boy. After Shon mentioned Alaska repeatedly over several years, I realized that this idea wasn't going away, even if he wasn't particularly fond of the cold.

Over the years, we talked about various places to live, but Alaska kept coming up. When Shon was eligible for retirement, he was a captain with the Aircraft Division of the Texas Department of Public Safety, and I was teaching math at a small charter school for at-risk students. Shon flew almost every day and knew he wanted aviation to continue to be a part of our lives. What better place to fly than Alaska? When Shon found the cabin at Cub Lake on an online real estate site, he had a feeling it was the perfect place for us. The peaceful solitude, rugged beauty, and the promise of flight resonated in our hearts. Life in Alaska appealed to both of us.

As soon as Shon was eligible for retirement, we planned a trip to Alaska.

CHAPTER 1

Difficult Decision

Cabin on Cub Lake

When my husband and I climbed in the little four-seat airplane for our first trip to the cabin on Cub Lake, we weren't sure what to expect. We were already taken by the rugged beauty of Alaska. We enjoyed a breathtaking tour of Denali by bush plane during the first part of our vacation and had seen breaching whales down on the Kenai from a ship. Now we were heading to the real reason for our trip: the cabin on Cub Lake. The cabin in the wilderness of Alaska seemed to have everything we wanted. It was remote, had a runway, and the scenery was postcard perfect. The pictures we had been poring over on the real estate site online were gorgeous. It had captured our imagination before we'd even left Texas. We were anxious to discover if it was too good to be true.

Walt, our pilot, loaded up the bush plane, and we headed out. We flew over forests of spruce and birch trees. As we got farther from the Willow Airport, we saw tall cottonwood trees along the banks of the Susitna River. We crossed over the braided river headed due west with Denali standing tall to the north. Shon and Walt chatted, but I didn't hear a word. The land was mesmerizing.

As we traveled further and further away from civilization, my excitement grew. After about twenty-five minutes of flight, the cabin at Cub Lake came into view. It was beautiful. Walt made a wide circle to let us get a look at the place. We descended over the lake and lined up on the 550-foot runway. As he slowed the plane, it almost looked like we were going to land in the lake. As we prepared for touch down, Walt cried, "Don't let me die!" Before I could even react to his crazy comment, the plane took a good bounce on the thirty-five-inch bush wheels and then rolled to a stop. I couldn't see out of the front of the aircraft, only out of the side, since I was in the back seat of the tailwheel aircraft (also known as a "taildragger"). I thought Walt had been showing off his skills by landing only halfway down the short dirt strip. When I climbed out of the plane, I found we were at the very end. I realized his comment, "Don't let me die!" might have only been half-joking. The next thing I noticed were wild strawberry plants growing on the runway. My heart was quickly being claimed by the last frontier.

We were unloading our bags when a bald man with a long, gray beard drove up. He was driving an old three-wheeler with two dogs following along, tails wagging. He and Walt visited a moment before introductions were made. Roger had lived across the lake with his dogs for the past four years. He was going to show us around and answer any questions about the place. As he shook my hand, I asked him if he was ready for neighbors. The last thing I wanted was to move in across the lake from some Alaskan recluse who hated people.

Walt and Shon on the way to Cub Lake

Cabin on Cub Lake, 2016

He thought about my question for a moment and replied, "I think I'm ready." As Walt flew away, we headed towards the house with our new friends Roger, Lilly, and Peanut.

As we toured the property and the house, we were amazed. Building a home on the road system with the hardware store around the corner was hard enough. How did someone get all of the supplies out here to build a 1600 square foot house, a functional shop, and a

9

guest cabin? The amount of time and effort it took to build a place like this, thirty miles from town as the crow flies, without a road, was mind-blowing. I couldn't imagine how the builder brought out the woodstove or the D3 Dozer. The place was fully furnished and had an incredible view of the snow-capped mountains of the Alaskan Range. After Roger gave us a brief tour, he left us to explore.

Shon and I looked over the property, enjoying the solitude. There was definitely work to do on the house, but the serenity of the place was unbelievable. Other than hearing a plane fly over occasionally, there were no other human sounds. While Shon looked in the shop more carefully, I got into the canoe that was at the lake's edge and quietly paddled out to the middle and looked back at the cabin. There were spruce trees all around the lake, swaying slowly in the breeze. Their reflection was almost perfect on the surface of the lake. Daisies, fireweed, and wild irises added a splash of color around the cabin. As I looked around and tried to take in all the beauty, I felt a calmness wash over me. I closed my eyes and took a deep breath of the fresh, clean air. I felt a peace that I'd never experienced before. I was safe.

Later that evening, Roger came back over with a couple of steaks for us to share. Shon put them on the grill that was on the front porch. I unpacked a few groceries I'd brought from town. I made a simple salad and mashed some potatoes, feeling at home in the small kitchen. As we sat down to eat, Shon prayed for God to bless our time together. As soon as the prayer was over, we started asking Roger questions. We asked him question after question about life in the wilderness. We had both lived out in the country as kids, but we had never lived off of the road system. And we had never lived without being connected to the power grid. This was all new to us. Roger patiently answered every question until late that evening.

Our new friend was an interesting character. Roger was quiet and didn't disclose much information without some prodding. I tried not to pry but was terribly curious about his life here. In our conversation that evening, I pieced together that he'd been living alone in the small, dry cabin across Cub Lake. He explained that he had bought his cabin, sight unseen, four years prior. He'd never stepped foot on Alaskan soil until he got off the plane from his flight from Colorado. As soon as he'd landed, he took a cab to the animal shelter and picked up Lilly, who had been his faithful friend since then. Walt had flown him, Lilly, and his few belongings out. Over the years, he had added Peanut, several chickens, and a little Chihuahua named Chachi to his homestead. It had been an adjustment living without running water and electricity, but he seemed to enjoy the serenity.

Ann with Roger from Cub Lake during the first trip, 2016

When Shon and I went to bed that night, we had a lot of information swirling in our heads. Roger was reserved, but friendly. And we were even more impressed with the cabin on Cub Lake than we thought we would be. I woke up during the night and tip-toed out to the front porch. As I listened to the sounds of the night, amazed at the beauty visible in the midnight sun, I asked God to direct our steps. I wasn't sure about the road ahead. As I slid back into bed later, I told myself not to rush into a decision. When I awoke the next morning, Shon was already up and out of bed. I heard him come in from outside and start the coffee. As I walked into the kitchen, I noticed a vase of daisies on the table that he had gathered for me. He had never picked flowers for me before, so I knew he was setting the stage. He was going to try to talk me into moving to this cabin in the wilderness of Alaska.

After our coffee and a simple breakfast, we walked around the property, considering our future. We talked about the isolation and the challenges of living so far from town. We discussed the cost of living. Shon mentioned that we would have to rely on ourselves more because we couldn't call a repairman or mechanic. Eating out would be a treat reserved only for rare trips to town. Having a cleaning lady was out of the question. And we would be a long way from the hospital if anything happened. Even with all of the challenges, it was easy to see the positives. We saw a place where we could grow together, draw near to God, and have an adventure of a lifetime.

Shon took my hands in his and said, "Honey, I need this." I knew he did, and I needed it, too. Shon's twenty-eight years in law enforcement and my years in public education had taken its toll on both of us. Our marriage had paid the price of dealing with other people's troubles and emergencies over the years. Finding this haven away from the world where we could let God heal our souls seemed like our only option. Standing on the dirt strip in the Alaskan wilderness, I noticed a look of hope in Shon's eyes that I hadn't seen since we first learned to fly. I remembered a promise I'd made to my husband when we were first married. I'd told him I would follow him anywhere. We had moved all over West Texas during our twenty-eight years of marriage. Here we were at a crossroads once again. Shon looked at me with a glint in his eye and said, "Follow me to Alaska!"

Preparing for the Big Move

In anticipation of moving to Alaska, we did everything we could to get ready for this possible change before we took the trip to Cub Lake. The first thing we did was ask God for his guidance. We got our Bibles out and started looking for some answers. There have been so many times when I wished God would say, "Move to Alaska" or "Don't do it!" but He doesn't seem to work that way. He wanted us to search. He has a way of laying things on our hearts and providing a way to find the answers to the questions we have. After much prayer and searching the Scriptures, one passage jumped out at us. We found 1 Thessalonians 4:11-12 (NIV), which says, "And to make it your ambition to lead a quiet life: You should mind your own business and work with your hands, just as we told you, so that your daily life may win the respect of outsiders and so that you will not be dependent on anybody." The fact that we *both* wanted this and that God had laid this on our hearts, we knew we had God's blessing. The more we searched and prayed, we were convinced that we not only had God's blessing, we had His calling.

Before retiring and following God's call, we had to get our finances in better shape. We got entirely out of debt except for two mortgages, our house and a rental. We set up a strict budget, which actually proved to be a great start to working together. It forced us to discuss our priorities. We realized that we should have created a budget years ago. We researched the cost of living in Alaska to make sure we weren't going to get in over our heads. The last thing we wanted to do was make a decision of this importance without considering the cost.

Many people move to Alaska without ever visiting first. We weren't that brave. We took sixteen days to see a small piece of the state in June of 2016. We did the typical sightseeing, but we were there to see if it was where we wanted to live. It was an awesome trip, and we had the opportunity to talk to many people about what life was like there. Going out to the cabin at Cub Lake was the highlight of our time in Alaska and was the deciding factor. On our way home, I started making lists of everything we had to get done to make this dream into a reality.

When we finally got home to El Paso after our trip, we had a lot to do. The first thing we did was talk to our kids. Without their support, we could not make this life-changing move. It wasn't going to affect just us. Knowing our boys, we figured they would be excited about our next adventure. We were right.

Jared

Jared, our youngest, graduated from high school the year before our trip to Alaska. He was working in a plumbing apprenticeship out of New Mexico. We saw him every other weekend, but each visit home was typically the same. He came in, asked what there was to eat, got a plate, and headed up to his room. He wasn't being disrespectful. He was going through the normal separation process that young adults invariably have to pass through. He was more interested in visiting with his friends than with his mom and dad. Even though I missed my little boy, I took this as a good sign that he was growing up. If we made the move, we would be a phone call away. It might take

14

us longer to get to him if needed, but we knew he was an extremely responsible young man for his age. It wasn't much different than children who move across the country for college, except that it was us moving away from our son. I knew it was going to be more difficult for me than anyone else, but God would see me through.

Jared's Senior Picture, 2015

As soon as we returned from our vacation, we sat down with Jared and told him about the rugged beauty of Alaska and the house on Cub Lake. We explained our desire to fly in Alaska and our need for some solitude. We finally broke down and told him we were considering a move up North. He was not surprised at all and readily gave his blessing. Later, when I asked him for the millionth time if he was sure, he took me by the shoulders, looked me in the eyes, and said, "Mom, this is no surprise to me. This is exactly who you and Dad are. You *have* to do this." He was our first supporter.

Kyle and Mirai

Kyle, our oldest son, was in the Army. He had returned to the States from Okinawa about six months before we started considering this move. He brought his new, beautiful wife, Mirai, with him. She was from Japan and had only been married to Kyle a little less than a year. Even though Mirai could understand and speak English, she was very quiet. I was excited about having a daughter-in-law and wanted to get to know her, but she didn't talk to me very much. Even with my best efforts, I could usually only get one- or two-word answers at a time. Needless to say, I did not know my Japanese daughter-in-law very well.

*Kyle and Mirai on one
of their first dates*

After finding an apartment and settling in El Paso, Kyle got word that he would be deploying to Qatar. We were all devastated, especially Mirai. Because of the immigration laws, she would need to remain in the US. She could not return to her family in Okinawa without jeopardizing her immigration status. The only people she knew living in El Paso were Shon and me. When the idea of moving to Alaska started to take shape in April, there was no way we were going to consider moving before Kyle returned home from deployment.

When we came home from our trip, we called and talked to Kyle about our experience up North. We told him that we were thinking of moving to the cabin on Cub Lake after he returned from deployment. A few days later, Kyle called us back. He asked us if we had considered moving right away. He thought we should ask Mirai to join us for the first leg of our adventure. We were shocked. Were we talking about this sweet girl who was too timid to even speak with us? Kyle said, "You might be surprised!" He agreed to talk with her about it to gauge her response. We didn't want her to feel obligated if we brought it up. Kyle called us right back and said, "Mirai is excited about joining you. You could move any time you want." Mirai was willing to move with us to an off-grid cabin in the middle of the Alaska wilderness. I didn't know Mirai well, but I was getting my first glimpse of her brave heart.

Are You *Crazy?*

I knew it was real when Shon called the Chief of the Aircraft Division to tell him that he would be retiring in August. I gave notice at my work as well. As we began to tell family and friends about our retirement plans, we got two very distinct reactions. Either people thought we were completely nuts or they were jealous that we were doing it instead of them.

There were definitely more people who thought we were crazy, and they did *not* mind telling us.

We got used to the reactions, but it was hard to hear that so many people thought we had lost our minds. I had to remind myself that they didn't know what I knew about our life. They didn't know how much we needed this change. They couldn't understand the call we felt from God to make this giant leap. We finally realized that we didn't have to explain ourselves to anyone. We decided that it was like any change in life. There are always people who try to tell us we are crazy for doing something different. We found out later that some people were even putting money into a pot, betting when we would give up and come home. It made us even more thankful for those who encouraged us along the way. And it strengthened our resolve to make this crazy move to the Alaskan wilderness successful.

Selling Our Possessions

Probably the most difficult for me, other than leaving family, was selling our belongings. We had twenty-eight years of accumulated possessions. I had been buying and selling antiques as a side business and had decorated our home with lots of beautiful pieces. I also had one-of-a-kind pieces of furniture passed down from grandparents and great grandparents. Parting with those sentimental items was tough. Most of the family heirlooms went to our kids, but everything had to go. We had an estate sale and sold all of our household goods. In July, we sold our house in El Paso and the rental that we owned in Alpine, making us completely debt-free. I cried, though, when my beloved Jeep sold. We sold it and our pickup truck. Shon even got rid of several guns, which had never happened in all our married life.

I packed thirty big totes with the items we thought we couldn't live without. We sent those thirty totes and Shon's long guns by first-class mail to Alaska. Everything else, we sold or gave away. Quite a few people suggested that we put our belongings in storage in case we ever came back. We considered that option but decided we didn't want one foot in Texas and one foot in Alaska. That was no way for us to live. Neither of us liked to do anything half-heartedly. If we were going to do this, we had to be all in.

It's Go Time

In sixty-seven days, we had reduced our lives to thirty totes. We no longer owned any property in Texas, but we were the proud owners of an off-grid, off-the-road-system cabin in the wilderness of Alaska. I was exhausted the morning Jared stopped by to take us to the airport. The house was completely empty except for our luggage. Mirai, quiet as always, was there with her two bags. Shon and Jared piled our bags into his truck as I locked the door for the last time. One chapter of my life was ending and another was beginning. We were making a huge leap and there was no turning back. We were leaving our house on a cul-de-sac in the city of El Paso to live alone in a cabin in the wilderness of Alaska. I thought I was ready for our Alaskan adventure to begin, but I had no clue of the ups and downs we had before us.

Leaving the house in El Paso for the last time, August, 2016

I will give you a new heart and put a new
spirit in you; I will remove from you your heart
of stone and give you a heart of flesh.

Ezekiel 36:26 NIV

19

CHAPTER 2

Moving North

Truck, Barge, and Side-by-Side

Mailing our totes to Alaska was the first part of our move. Getting our household goods to the cabin on Cub Lake was the next step. We decided we would have a barge take our things up the Yentna River and unload on the riverbank. Then Roger, our new neighbor, would get Shon there in an old Argo, an eight-wheeled, all-terrain vehicle. They would pick up our Arctic Cat side-by-side so we could start the process of getting our belongings the three miles to the house. Shon called about a barge and made arrangements with Larry, a well-known Alaskan who had been barging for decades. After adding up our expenses, we decided this was going to be a pretty inexpensive move, compared to our last few moves across Texas. We were set and ready to go.

This was going to be a piece of cake!

Shon, Mirai, and I left El Paso, Texas, on August 22nd, 2016. We each had two bags of personal items. We got off of the plane in

Anchorage, took a bus to a hotel, and woke up ready for our Alaskan adventure that next morning. We didn't have time to stand in awe of the majestic mountains. We hit the ground running. We took a taxi to the U-Haul place, where we had reserved a U-Haul van. We picked up a grocery order that I had put in from a wholesale store. I ordered enough canned goods to last us at least a month, along with flour, beans, rice, and other staples for six months or more. We had made a list of all of the things that we thought we needed to survive in the Alaska bush. We went around that day and bought supplies, including $400 worth of meat and other groceries that we stored in two large coolers. Around noon we headed to Wasilla to get our totes and guns from our real estate agent, Carrie. She was not in town, but she gave us directions to her house where all of our things were piled in her garage. She was gracious enough to offer us to stay in her home if we needed to while getting things done. There was no need—or so I thought. We had this move planned down to the minute. No detail had escaped us.

With all of our worldly possessions in the back of the U-Haul, we headed to Deshka Landing, a few miles from Willow. We were meeting a guy who had an Arctic Cat all-terrain vehicle for sale. It had both tires and tracks and seemed to be just what we needed for our life in the bush. He was there waiting, just like he said. We made the deal, and he agreed to haul it to the barge so we could have it loaded.

It was about this time when I told Shon and Mirai that I was so pleasantly surprised that everything was going as planned. We intended to unload our stuff on the barge and then return the U-Haul to Wasilla, where Walt's wife was going to pick us up. She had planned to take us back to Willow, and then Walt would fly us out to our new home. We would be there by early evening. Shon and

Roger would meet the barge the next day, and we would be settled into our new home lickety-split.

But that is not what happened.

We drove up to Larry's trailer house at Deshka Landing. Mirai and I got out of the van to look over the new Arctic Cat side-by-side while Shon went in to make arrangements to use the barge. Shon had been calling Larry throughout the last few weeks to make sure everything was lined up for our move and had talked to him that morning before we left the hotel. Mirai and I waited and waited with the guy who had sold us the side-by-side. I wondered why he was sticking around and chalked it up to Alaskans being so friendly and helpful. Looking back, I think he just wanted to see what was going to happen next to these crazy Texans. Shon was in the house longer than I felt comfortable. I was beginning to think that something had gone wrong and asked Mirai to stay out with "Arctic Cat Man" while I went in and checked on things.

The first thing I noticed when I walked in the house was the oxygen bottle. I also caught a glimpse of Larry and his wife. There were tubes from the oxygen bottle to Larry's nose, and he was a deathly shade of gray. His wife looked distraught. It is hard to explain the look on Shon's face. He doesn't get upset often, so I'm not entirely sure how to describe what I saw. I think it might have been a look of devastation if Shon was even capable of that emotion. I heard Shon tell him that he had the coordinates to the drop off location, and Larry replied, "I don't use that new GPS stuff. Honey, get the phone, so I can call around and find out exactly where this drop-off place is on the Twenty-Mile Slough."

I found out shortly that Larry had had a pacemaker put in *the day before* and wasn't supposed to be working. Being a strong, stubborn

Alaskan man, he must have thought he was invincible. He took off the tubes from the oxygen bottle, stood up, and announced that we would get the barge loaded. I had a moment of hope. We trudged outside and he pulled up the door on our U-Haul. Apparently, he and Shon had not communicated well about the number of things we were expecting him to barge down the river. Shon had told him we needed to haul all of our personal belongings, but somewhere along the way, that was lost in the communications. With the side-by-side, our thirty-one totes, the long guns, and extra supplies that we had gathered that day in a mad rush, we had a substantial load that seemed to be more than Larry expected. He shook off his surprise and told us we would need to get it unloaded under a shed so it wouldn't get rained on, and then he would load it all onto the barge the next day. We started cleaning out a place under a shed while Larry got a forklift ready.

I looked over, and Larry was looking worse and worse. Shon and I had the same thought at the same time. This wasn't going to work. Larry was going to die, trying to barge our things down the river right after his surgery. We voiced our concerns as gently as possible, and Larry finally agreed. He just couldn't do it, as much as he wanted to try.

So there we were, swatting mosquitoes, trying to figure out our Plan B. Larry decided to call in some backup and contacted a young freighter, Jody. He was interested in the job and arrived in a pickup truck a few minutes later. He took a look at our stuff, gave an estimate of the price for barging it up the river, but said he couldn't do it for a couple of days. We would have to keep the load in the U Haul and meet him a couple of days later. I was ecstatic and Shon was relieved. I still couldn't tell how Mirai felt about any of it. "Arctic Cat Man" seemed genuinely relieved that we weren't going to try to get our money back from him so we could head back to Texas, but he also seemed reluctant to head back home to Fairbanks.

We put the Arctic Cat under the shed that we had just cleaned out and drove back to Wasilla to stay at the real estate agent's house. I had assured her over the phone that we would only be in her home a couple of nights at most. I canceled the charter flight with Walt and notified our soon-to-be neighbor, Roger, of our change in plans. That night when we finally got to sleep after such an exhausting day, my phone rang. It was our new friend, "Arctic Cat Man", letting us know that he had made it back to Fairbanks safely. I laid there wide awake, wondering about the strange call. I didn't think we would ever see this man again (I didn't even know his name) and couldn't understand why he'd called. As I considered the events of the day, I asked myself what in the world we were thinking when we had decided to move to Alaska. We might just be crazy after all.

Larry to the Rescue

Carrie, our real estate agent, went above and beyond by extending an invitation to use her home. She had a friend, Vicki, staying at her house as well, who was watching after the animals. She was such an encouragement to us. Vicki told us about her experience coming to Alaska. She understood that strong desire to move to this beautiful, wild place. It was refreshing to talk to her, since we had just left many friends and family in the lower forty-eight who thought we had absolutely lost our minds. People usually don't know what a simple act of kindness can do, but Vicki did something really sweet for me. I absolutely loved my plants back in Texas, but there was no way for me to bring them to Alaska. Without even knowing that, Vicki offered some plant cuttings to me. I was so thrilled to get those two plants. I put them in water right away and just hoped there were some planters out in my new home where they could grow. Vicki and I hit it off right away, and I really enjoyed visiting with her, getting as much information about Alaska as I could.

Because we had a cooler full of meat and it was going to be a couple of extra days before getting into the house, we took advantage of Carrie's offer to "make ourselves at home." We put the meat into her freezer. I went through all of the groceries and put all of the perishables in the second cooler. We took the extra days to unbox, organize, and prioritize our load. We also had a chance to go over our many lists, get a few more needed supplies, and rest up before the big move. This was actually a good thing. This was just what we needed. We kept in close contact with Roger, letting him know how things were progressing. He was looking forward to our arrival, and his only concern was the rain. Shon and I weren't too worried about it. It was just a drizzle.

We were now packed up more efficiently and were more ready than ever. We were going to meet Jody, our new freighter, the next day and begin our new life in Alaska. That night, Shon got a call. Jody had an engine blow on his barge and wouldn't be able to take our load after all. I couldn't hear the conversation but could tell by the look on Shon's face that all was not well. When he got off the phone, Shon assured me that Jody was trying to figure out a Plan C. In just a few terrifying moments, we got another call. We were back on with Larry. *What?* Larry had two small barges. We would load up both barges. Larry would take one, and Jody would take the other. Larry had had a couple more days to recover from *heart surgery*, so he would be fine. I didn't want to fall apart in front of my daughter-in-law. She was looking to us, trusting that we had everything under control, so Shon and I hid our fears and embraced Plan C. We would officially start our move out to the bush the next day.

When we got back out to Larry's, I noticed the same shade of gray on Larry's face. He still didn't look like he had recovered. His wife, Lucille, was there with the same worried look. He had already gotten both barges up to the house where we would be loading. We pulled our U-Haul up to the side of the barge so it would be easy to transfer the load. Our totes were about fifty pounds each. Shon was in the U-Haul and I was in the barge. He handed me one tote at a time, and I started stacking them in the barge for the trip up the river. In just a bit, Larry was moving me out of the way. He just couldn't stand seeing me struggle with those heavy totes. He should not have done it, but it was amazing to see him sling those heavy totes into the barge like they were nothing. Did I mention that he was a tough old bird?

Loading all that we owned onto one of the barges

27

The first barge going into the water,
Deshka Landing, August of 2016

I voiced my concerns but they fell on deaf ears. Things changed, though, when Larry's wife came out to see about him. She was a small woman, but she looked like she could hold her own with her tough Alaskan husband. He immediately stopped what he was doing, and it was evident that it was my turn with the totes. His wife was not fooled. "Larry! You shouldn't be doing that," she scolded.

"I'm not doing anything," he replied.

"Then why are you wearing those work gloves?" she countered.

He thought for just a moment. "My hands are cold!" he exclaimed.

Lucille gave me a look that said I needed to help her keep him from killing himself. When she went back into the house, he started grabbing totes, but I hung in there and got as many as I possibly could, even though I had a hard time keeping up with him. Larry Heater had my respect. And his wife had my sympathy.

28

It was exciting when we had the totes packed, the Arctic Cat loaded, everything covered with tarps, and we were finally on our way to our new home. Not only had Larry done such an excellent job with Plan C, but he also gave us gas cans that he was not using and wrapped my sewing table up in one of his sleeping bags so it wouldn't get scratched. He told us that we looked like we really prepared for our new life. His words were very encouraging. He told us to get our food moved first so we wouldn't attract any hungry bears. I was glad we had had the time to reorganize. Our belongings were in good hands and would be delivered onto the riverbank the next day around noon. He knew right where to go and was looking forward to the trip. I think he was ready to get out of the house and away from the watchful eye of his sweet wife. We were tired and hungry, but in good spirits when we left Larry's place.

As we were leaving Deshka Landing, we stopped at the gate. We went in the store there to thank Amy, the gatekeeper, for letting us in and allowing us to use the dock. We visited a few minutes. She asked some of the same questions that we were getting used to answering. After we responded to her questions about where we were going to live, she surprised us by saying, "Well, good luck to ya! If you guys make it out there, you will be the first ones this year!" Shon and I looked at each other, stunned. I was desperately hoping Mirai hadn't heard what she'd said. We refused to let those words dampen our spirits as we drove to Willow to catch the charter flight out to our new home.

Walt was ready for us when we arrived in Willow. We had very little with us, since we had unloaded most of our belongings onto the barge. We had each packed enough clothes for a couple of days and I had a few groceries to tide us over until we got our supplies from the river. I did have my two new plants on my lap, wrapped loosely in wet paper towels. My heart soared as we took off toward our new home. The trip was stunning, and I enjoyed watching Mirai take pictures with her phone as we neared the house, a clue that she was enjoying her adventure.

How can one person have so much excitement and fear all mixed up at once? We had faced obstacles in our move and had figured it out. God would not have put this longing in our hearts if He wasn't with us. We were going to be okay. We were off by a few days. We would get to our new home, get our belongings from the river, and start getting wood for winter. Life was good. I just needed to ignore the words, "If you guys make it, you will be the first ones this year" that were echoing in my brain.

Shon's First Trip to the River

I was excited when my eyes first came open that first morning in our new home. I hopped up and got breakfast so Shon would be ready for his trip to the river. Roger came over at about ten a.m. so they could start the process of moving our household goods. They were scheduled to meet Larry and Jody at the top of the Twenty-Mile Slough at around one p.m.

The slough was a channel that snaked around away from the main Yentna River for about twenty miles before being reconnected. On the river, the Twenty-Mile Slough was a recognizable landmark. The top of the slough was farther downriver, whereas the bottom of the slough was considered the part closer to town. They took off in the Argo with a small, wooden trailer turned upside down in a metal meat wagon, an aluminum trailer used to haul moose. The dogs, Lilly and Peanut, were following happily behind them. Roger thought the trail to the river was about eight miles, but it had been a while since he'd been down it.

After they got away from the house, Shon was surprised. Our house was built on a hill on good ground, but just a little ways from our home was muskeg. The muskeg was swampy, almost spongy. The muskeg was full of small ponds, some deeper than others. Shon and Roger stayed near the trees where the ground was better. From time to time, they had to navigate between the little ponds. After about an hour of traversing the muskeg, they came to a seismic line. Back in the 1960s many trails were made in this country for oil exploration. These seismic lines are used as makeshift roads for many people out in the bush. The trail was overgrown with willows. There were places on hills that were on good ground, but there were also low, muddy spots. The trail was very narrow, and as they traveled down this straight path, the willows continually hit them as they drove along. They got stuck three times on the seismic trail and had to use the come-along to get unstuck. Shon and Roger were both covered with mud. It took them three hours to reach the river. It was much more difficult than Shon ever imagined it would be.

As Shon and Roger neared the river, they saw Jody walking down a runway near our drop-off location. He was checking out the area while waiting for Shon to arrive. They discussed where our household goods were to be unloaded. Larry pulled one of the barges to the bank and lowered the ramp on the front to the ground. Shon drove the Arctic Cat off of the barge, and then they unloaded the rest of our supplies. Jody did the same with the second barge, and all of our earthly possessions were plopped on the river's edge in the middle of nowhere, Alaska. Larry and Jody turned back towards town while Shon and Roger prepared for the difficult trek back to the cabin.

They pulled the wooden trailer off of the meat wagon and hooked it to the Arctic Cat. They loaded it with one cooler of food along with several five-gallon buckets full of beans, rice, and other staples. They also loaded another cooler into the meat wagon along with other food items. The goal was to get as much food as possible back to the cabin before it spoiled or attracted bears.

Larry and Jody on a barge

It didn't take Shon long to realize that the wooden trailer was not going to be useful. It had skinny tires that sank deep into the mud. The mud piled up in front, making the trailer difficult to pull. It was like dragging a refrigerator through the mud. They had more trouble on the return trip than they did on their journey to the river. Their boots were full of muck and they were covered from head to toe with bits of muskeg. They used the come-along to get unstuck four or five more times. When they finally got home, around nine p.m., they only had the Argo and one cooler of food. And it was the wrong cooler. The meat cooler and everything else they had with them was left on the trail, stuck deep in the mud. I had visions of bears feasting on our supply of meat. They were probably laughing at us, thanking their lucky stars for naïve Texans who try to move to Alaska.

Stuck, Stuck, and Stuck Again

It is incredible what a good night's rest will do to restore my soul. We woke up, and I peppered Shon with questions about the trip to the river. He had a hard time putting it into words. He just kept saying, "I can't explain it." I didn't understand. How hard could the eight-mile trail be? I had been four-wheeling in Texas. I sold a Jeep to come here. We had taken that Jeep on some really rough trails outside of El Paso. We weren't wimps. It was eight lousy miles. I was frustrated with his lack of answers and stomped to the kitchen to make the coffee. I made breakfast with some of the provisions I'd brought from town on the airplane, but those supplies were running thin. We really needed to get the rest of our food from the river, if the bears hadn't already eaten it all. Mirai woke up with her usual sunny-but-quiet disposition. Roger showed up after breakfast with his little Chihuahua, Chachi, and he and Shon started making a plan while Mirai played with the little dog.

After some discussion, the guys decided they would head back to the river, get the Arctic Cat unstuck on the way, take it back to the river where they would put the tracks on, then bring back two loads. Roger would carry a load in his Argo and the meat trailer, and Shon would bring the Arctic Cat pulling the wooden trailer. They told me that they might not make it back that same day. They were prepared to spend the night out on the trail if they had to, so I agreed to be patient. I had instructions to call Walt or the State Police if they weren't back by the following night. This was going to take time if they were going to do it right. Mirai and I were babysitting Chachi until Roger got back. Lilly and Peanut were going with them to the river for bear patrol. I was scared, but there was nothing I could do but wait for their return.

Roger in the Argo

The sun was shining as they left on their second trip to the river. Mirai and I kept ourselves busy that day, trying not to worry. We pulled everything out of the kitchen cabinets so we could do a deep clean. No one had lived in the house for several years, and it showed. We rearranged some of the furniture to make it feel more like home. It was strange moving into someone else's house with someone else's furniture. As we cleaned the house, I took stock of what items were there and started making a list of what we would need to get in town on our next trip. I found myself looking out of the window many times during the day, hoping to see Shon. My mood changed as the day wore on.

By evening, fear had completely taken over, but I was trying to appear brave for Mirai. Dusk turned to night, and they still hadn't returned. Mirai and I finally went to bed, praying for their safety. Chachi insisted on sleeping with me, so he was some comfort. I lay there in the strange surroundings, wondering what in the world we had gotten ourselves into. This cabin that had promised peace and tranquility was only delivering fear. I was almost convinced that Shon had been torn to bits by a grizzly bear when I heard the Argo. It was almost midnight, but they had made it home.

I jumped up, changed my clothes, and ran downstairs as they were pulling up to the back of the cabin. The Arctic Cat was nowhere in sight, but Shon was there with Roger in the Argo. Roger climbed out, fell on the ground, and exclaimed, "That sucked!" I wanted to ask a million questions but realized that it was not the right time. They were covered in mud, as was everything in the back of the Argo. We unloaded what little they had brought in the dark, and Roger drove home with Chachi wrapped up in a blanket under one arm, exhausted. They had gotten the meat cooler and a few other supplies, but that was it. I was disappointed and relieved all at once. I was so glad they had made it back safely but was shocked that after a fourteen-hour day, we had little to show for it. If we continued at this rate, we would never get all of our belongings.

As Shon climbed into bed, he told me they got the Arctic Cat back to the river and put the tracks on. It did okay on the trail, but they were still getting stuck every mile or so, especially in the seismic trails. Instead of having one vehicle getting stuck, they now had two with trailers, and it was really slowing them down. When it started getting late, they decided to leave the Arctic Cat and the two trailers on the trail and travel in the Argo so they could get home for the night. They planned to return the next day to get it all. Things would go quicker the next day, because they didn't have to go all the way to the river. After that, we would get the kinks worked out with the Arctic Cat on tracks, and we could get the rest of our belongings. I knew Shon had done his very best. I finally went to sleep, thankful for Shon lying next to me but wondering what the future would bring.

The next day was a short, successful day. Shon and Roger were back by five with the Arctic Cat and two trailer loads. We were so happy to have the guns, the chainsaw, and several totes. I was also relieved to have some more of our food, but I was super excited to get into the totes. I needed items from my previous life to help me feel normal. I opened the first one only to find all of our financial and tax papers. That tote didn't help me at all, but the next one was full of pictures. Mirai picked several photos out of that tote and hung them on a bulletin board that was hanging in the dining room. It was beginning to feel like we were going to make it. My joy turned to dread, however, when Shon told me that I would be riding shotgun on the next trip to the river. Roger was done.

My First Trip to the River

I was up bright and early the next morning, determined to take my turn to the river. As I gathered the supplies that we needed to be gone for the day, Shon looked over the Arctic Cat. I was loading things in the back when he told me we couldn't go. The axle on the rear of the Arctic Cat was broken and needed to be replaced. Getting it fixed would require a trip to town. Shon called Walt, our air taxi pilot, to schedule a pick up when he could fit him in. Late that afternoon, Shon left with Walt for his quick trip. When he took the axle in, they thought they could fix it in just an hour or so, but called Shon later to tell him that it was shot and they needed to order a new one. I was terribly disappointed when he came home with just a few bags from the store, but no axle. We didn't get the replacement for a week and a half, which was plenty of time for me to get nervous about my first trip to the river.

Shon working on the Arctic Cat

Shon still working on the Arctic Cat, Fall of 2016

After Walt finally dropped off the part and Shon put it on, we were ready to go get another load. The temperatures were getting colder each day, so I dressed in several layers. I took food and water while Shon put in all of the supplies that he knew we were going to need if we had trouble with the tracks or if we got stuck. We left Mirai at the house with instructions to call Roger if she needed help.

We weren't even a mile from the house when one of the tracks came off. The inside of the track had teeth that kept it aligned with a series of small wheels. We had trouble with the track and small wheels getting out of line. To fix it, we had to jack the vehicle up to get the pressure off of the track. We took a couple of the little wheels off to get everything realigned. After retightening everything, we were ready to go again. The process had gotten a lot quicker. We could get one back on correctly in about thirty minutes instead of the hour that it had taken us when we'd first started.

After having to stop one more time to repeat the process, we discussed our dilemma. We needed to look at the tracks every few minutes to see if they were staying aligned. If we caught the problem before it was too bad, we might save some time. I hung out of my side of the Arctic Cat every few minutes to take a good look at the passenger-side tracks. Shon did the same on his side, which was a bit trickier because he was still driving. We finally broke out of the woods next to a beautiful lake, which Shon informed me was Serene Lake. The land flattened out along the bank and there were spruce trees from time to time, but the land was completely different from the wooded, hilly area that we had just come from. I felt pretty good about getting through this first portion of the trail, and I asked Shon if that was the worst of it. He looked at me funny and shook his head no.

I thought for sure that the tracks would do better now that we weren't hitting them against logs and rocks along the winding trail. This portion of the trail was muskeg, a wet, spongy ground. We traveled along about ten miles per hour, hanging out of our respective sides of the Arctic Cat to watch for any sign of those teeth and wheels getting out of line. We hadn't gone far when Shon stopped the vehicle. The rear drivers-side track was off.

Shon got out all of the supplies and got to work. I knew what I needed to do to help: stay out of the way and not ask too many questions. When he went to jack up the Arctic Cat in the muskeg, the jack just sank deeper and deeper in the wet, mossy soil. We weren't getting anywhere, so Shon took his chainsaw and walked fifty yards or so to a tree and cut it down. He cut a portion out of it and brought it back to where I was waiting. He used the wood under the jack to keep it from sinking so much, and we finally saw some progress. Thirty minutes later, we were back on our way. We had been on the trail for about two hours and had made it about two and a half miles. Again, I asked Shon if this was the worst part of the trail. Once again, he looked at me funny and shook his head no.

Shon had only been down this trail three times, and there were places where the trail basically disappeared. Roger had tied trail tape to some of the trees along the route, so I watched for the pink ribbon as I continued my job of checking the tracks every few minutes. Shon also had a GPS that he was checking to make sure we didn't get lost. Everything looked the same to me. There were small clumps of spruce trees. In other places, there were low hills where we could see birch and spruce trees around the perimeter. Mostly we saw water—lots and lots of water. There were little ponds and lakes everywhere. The trail wound around the ponds and then headed toward the next small clump of trees where the ground was a little more reliable. Driving next to the ponds was frightening to me. We were super close. I had a fear that we were going to tip over into one of those ponds and I had no idea how deep they were.

We were going through a particularly nasty portion of the muskeg when I did my track-check. The track hadn't gotten out of line—*the whole assembly had come off* and was turned at a funny angle. It reminded me of a broken leg. I started screaming for Shon to stop, but he didn't. He gunned it to make it through the squashy muskeg to a better portion of land before taking care of what he thought was another misaligned track. By the time he stopped, I didn't know how much damage might have been done. It looked horrible. I thought for sure that it was damaged beyond repair.

Here we were in the middle of nowhere. I was mad because Shon hadn't stopped when I was screaming for him to stop. My adrenaline was pumping, and I was panic-stricken and tired and frustrated. I had never felt more defeated in my entire life. I sat down in my seat, numb. Shon was looking at it all, seeing why the thing had decided to come off. He realized that the nuts that had held the mechanism in place backed off, and we lost them on the trail. Shon looked around for them, but they were long gone. He tightened the others, which were also loose, while he considered our options. I sat in my seat and pouted. I had no hope. In just a bit, he came running over with a big smile on his face, and he said, "I have more nuts!"

Arctic Cat Man had given Shon extra nuts in a baggy. Shon had thrown them in the back of the side-by-side and completely forgotten about them. There they were, ready to save us from a long walk back home through the muskeg, but I refused to get my hopes up. I sat there thinking that Shon and I were both nuts for making this crazy move. What the heck were we thinking? I didn't feel much better after Shon had everything back on and proved to me that it was entirely fixed. It had not been damaged, and we were good to go. I begrudgingly started my job of checking the tracks and looking for trail tape as we resumed our ten-mph trek down the trail once again, but I was *not* happy about it. We weren't even halfway to the river yet.

Shon had tried to explain what the seismic trails were like. He said they were muddy, and the willows draped over the narrow path. He hadn't been exaggerating. There was no way I could hang out of the side-by-side to do my track-check. The willows were so thick that I couldn't get out. Even if I could, I wouldn't be able to see the tracks. They were covered with mud at least halfway up. When we entered the seismic trail, the mud started inching up towards our floorboards. If I had to stand in that mud, it would have come up to my knee in places. The willows slapped my legs and my arms. Shon hollered at me to cover my eyes, fearful that I would get an eye poked out. I covered them but wondered how he was driving if he had his eyes covered, too. From time to time, I would peek out with my head turned towards him to see how he was doing. Shon had his left arm up, protecting his face while trying to keep the Arctic Cat going down the trail. He didn't dare stop, or we would be stuck for sure. I started praying out loud for God to be with us. I knew Shon couldn't hear me over the whine of the engine and the sound of the branches hitting us and the windshield, but I knew God would listen to my cries for help. I didn't have to ask Shon if this was the worst part of the trail. I knew it was. I couldn't imagine it getting any worse than this.

At the end of that three-mile stretch of seismic trail, there was an old pickup truck. How or why it was there, I had no idea, but I was delighted to see it that day, and even happier to be out of the willows. Right after passing the old vehicle, we made a turn out onto a beautiful, lush runway. We had made it to the river! Shon showed me where he and Roger had moved all of our belongings from the muddy river bank and had stacked them under a shed, out of the rain. The shed and runway were owned by a sweet couple, Mike and Patti, who resided in Wasilla. I got their telephone number from Larry as soon as Shon and Roger realized that getting our belongings from the river to our house was going to be a challenge. I called to ask if it was okay with them if we stacked our belongings under their shed, out of the weather. Mike told me to leave our stuff there as long as we needed. He even suggested that we wait for winter so we could travel down the trail on a pogo stick. I reassured him that we had it under control, and we would have our stuff out from under his shed in short order. I appreciated his patience with us, but I hadn't enjoyed the crack about the pogo stick. Now that I was here to see it all for myself, I was so thankful for that shed and their willingness to let us use it.

Shon and I looked over our pile, trying to decide what needed to go first. After some discussion, we loaded some of our supplies into the wooden trailer that we had brought along. We talked about eating the lunch that we had with us, but decided we didn't have the time. We drank a bottle of water while we loaded the trailer with a couple of totes. We piled some plywood on top of the totes and cinched it all down. It didn't look like much of a load, so I grabbed a bag of clothes and put them by my feet in the Arctic Cat. We needed to get as much as possible if it was going to be this much work. With our load secured, we headed back down the muddy path towards home.

I started praying while Shon plowed through the mud. It was more difficult now that we had a small load. We weren't too far from the old truck when we were stuck. I didn't dare get out of the vehicle. Shon jumped out and gathered up the come-along. He explained that he was going to find an appropriate tree to connect it to and then would hook it to the Arctic Cat as well. Shon would slowly pull the Arctic Cat out of the hole it was in. At that point, he would need me to drive the Arctic Cat up the trail a little way to a hill where the mud wasn't as deep. Shon explained that if I stopped before getting out of the deep mud, we would have to repeat the process. I climbed over to the driver's side while he did what he needed to do. I was intimidated but decided that I had to do this. When the time was right, he gave me the signal. I punched it, mud flew, and I drove out of the mud like a boss. I let out a crazy yell when I made it to the designated spot without losing my bag of clothes from the passenger's seat. Shon kissed me big on the lips and we started down the trail once again.

There are times when I think God knows that we have had enough for one day. We only got stuck that one time in the seismic trail. The rest of the way home, we didn't lose a track. We got back to the house around seven p.m., tired to the core. Overall, it was a successful trip. We just needed to use the meat wagon instead of the wooden trailer. That would make all of the difference in the world. We would get a more significant load, and it wouldn't bog us down in the mud as much. We survived the day and were ready to try this moving thing again. We were really getting the hang of it now.

Bridge over Cripple Creek

The next time we went to the river, we were beginning to work together better. He had his jobs and I had mine. We were feeling pretty good when we got to the halfway mark on the trail, which was a small creek. Shon and Roger had built a narrow bridge over the stream so we could drive over it with our side-by-side. The bridge was made out of logs laid across the creek. On top of the logs, they nailed milled slabs of wood that went perpendicular to the logs to create a nice little homemade bridge. It was strong enough, but not very wide. When we got to the bridge, I asked to get out. I thought it might be best if I walked over the bridge and got in the Arctic Cat on the other side of the creek. I might be adventurous, but I wasn't sure about that narrow bridge. Shon agreed, so he stopped and let me out. He lined up on the bridge and asked me if it looked like he was straight. Before I could even answer, he gunned it and hurried across the bridge with no trouble. I was impressed.

We made it all of the way to Mike and Patti's place this particular trip by about two p.m. We were stoked. We hooked up the meat wagon and loaded it down with about 300 pounds of canned goods and totes and other supplies. We smiled at each other as we made the turn at the old truck and headed back down the trail. This was the adventure of a lifetime. Who else gets to move to their new home down a muddy seismic trail driving a side-by-side? We were finally going to get a good load. We could do this. We only got stuck a couple of times, but got out with the help of the come-along. We had our system down pretty well. Shon used the come-along to pull us out of the hole, and I drove out of the mud.

All was going well until we got to the bridge.

Again, I asked to get out and walk across the bridge while Shon did the brave work of driving over with our precious load. We had already done this once. What could go wrong? Shon was in the side-by-side, and the meat wagon was behind him at a slight angle. When he gunned the side-by-side to get over the bridge, the meat wagon, now loaded down with supplies, pulled the rear end of the side-by-side over about a foot. It was just enough to cause the back track to slide completely off the bridge. I thought Shon was a goner. The Arctic Cat tipped over so much that I thought it was going over on its side. The only reason it didn't tip over was because it was still attached to the loaded down trailer. Shon flew out of the Arctic Cat and landed on his feet in the creek. If it had tipped over, it would have crushed Shon. I will never forget the look on his face.

After we got ourselves calmed down, we had to figure out how to get the side-by-side out of the creek, or we would be walking the four miles back to the house. Through the muskeg. In the dark. With the bears and the wolves.

The Arctic Cat off of the bridge at Cripple Creek

Shon unhooked the trailer with all of our load to free the side-by-side. Shon got the chainsaw out and started cutting the bridge out while I started looking at all of the angles, trying to figure out how we could use the come-along to get us out of this mess. I was scared to death Shon was going to cut the gas tank of the Arctic Cat while cutting out the bridge, but he never did. We had to move the come-along several times while pulling the Arctic Cat this way and that, but after about three hours, we finally got the thing out. Our mood was a little sour the rest of the way to the house. When we got back, all we had to show for our day's work was a trash bag full of clothes and a package of lightbulbs.

We had to go back to Cripple Creek, my new name for the dangerous stream, the next day to rebuild the bridge. We cut down spruce trees and dragged them over to the creek. I made sure that the bridge was a bit wider this go-around. It took us all day. When we were finished, there sat the meat wagon, loaded down. We didn't dare go across the bridge to retrieve it with the Arctic Cat. We hooked up the come-along to the meat wagon on one side of the bridge. We walked across the bridge and attached the other end of the come-along to our Arctic Cat on our side of the bridge. Slowly and carefully, we pulled our load across our newly built bridge. As soon as it was across, we breathed a sigh of relief, hooked the meat wagon to our Arctic Cat, and headed home. That was the most significant load we got from the river. And everything we brought back, including ourselves, were covered with mud.

Our rebuilt bridge at Cripple Creek

Five-Hour Yuck Muck

We did get smarter. We waited a few weeks. We were patient. What we were doing wasn't working, so we had to modify our plan. Autumn was upon us and the temperatures were freezing at night, so the land would be better for traveling. The mud would be thicker. The muskeg would be harder. We also decided we needed to leave much earlier in the morning, before the warmer temperatures would start melting everything. Once more, we gathered up our supplies and headed towards the river. We knew the trail well by this time. We knew just what to avoid, so we wouldn't lose a track. We still lost one from time to time, but we had learned how to put a track back on in less than half an hour. We could do this.

We rounded a corner at about six a.m. in the dark with only our headlights to guide us. We saw a snowshoe hare dart out in front of us, which made us laugh. This was going to be a good day. I buckled my seat belt because I had seen Shon almost get dumped out of the side-by-side on the bridge and didn't want to take any chances. I was dressed in several layers because it was really cold. Shon had done the same. We got to Serene Lake, about a mile and a half from the house, when we ran into a bit of trouble. We drove off into a mud hole right next to the lake. Shon put the Arctic Cat in reverse and backed us right out of it. I was so relieved. My relief turned to terror when he put it in gear, picked up speed, and hit that mud hole with as much force as he could. He thought we could go through it. We didn't.

We had broken through the muskeg and were actually under the ground. When we hit that wall of muskeg and mud, it tipped us over to the right. We were submerged in mud up over the floorboards, and I was tilted close to the lake and muck. Shon's side of the Arctic Cat was sitting up higher. I was still buckled in and was afraid that I was going to drown. I screamed and hollered, trying to get unbuckled and away from what looked to be a certain death. Shon had to help me climb up on his side of the Arctic Cat while he was climbing out into the mud on his side. Some harsh words might have been said at this point.

5 Hour Yuck Muck

It took us five hours to get the Arctic Cat out of that deep hole. We used two come-alongs at two separate angles and Roger's Argo to pull us out. Every time we would get it out of the mud a little bit, we pushed small trees that we had cut down under the track on the passenger side to try to get it to sit up level. I was no fan of the Arctic Cat and cursed the day we purchased the thing. I also had a few choice words for Arctic Cat Man. I'm pretty sure his ears were burning that day, and many days to come.

Death Shroud

Summer was gone and we were in full-fledged fall. Temperatures continued to drop, and the ground began to freeze. Shon and I thought that the Arctic Cat might just make it to the river, since the mud had a thick crust on it. We decided to give it one more try, because we desperately needed our supplies.

We left the house as soon as there was a bit of light. We had all of the supplies that we needed in case we had trouble: chainsaw, come-along, high-lift jack, boards, large screwdriver, grease gun, hammer, and a tarp. We were dressed warmly. I had on long johns, pants, a ski suit, a heavy outer jacket, waterproof boots, and warm gloves. We said a quick prayer for safety and headed out once more.

We made it about a mile into the muskeg when we started breaking through the frozen ground down into the muck. Even though things were going reasonably well and we hadn't had to stop to fix one of the tracks, we knew it wasn't going to work. If we were breaking through, we would never make it through the several miles of mud on the seismic line. We decided to turn around and head home before we got ourselves into trouble. I got out of the Arctic Cat and stood to the side while Shon found a place to turn around. When he finally got us headed back towards the house, I jumped back in.

We were disappointed that the ground wasn't frozen enough, but were somewhat proud of ourselves for making this reasonable decision together. It just wasn't worth the risk, and we could try another day. We were rocking along the trail a couple of miles from home when the side-by-side stopped. The tracks were on, but the vehicle would not move forward. What was wrong now? Shon took the cover off of the motor and found that the belt had worn through. We were done.

I cannot tell you how defeated we were at that moment. We had these big plans to live in Alaska, and we couldn't even get our stuff moved to the house. We questioned our decision but knew without a doubt that we were following God's leading. Why was this so hard? I hated that Arctic Cat and all of the trouble it had caused us. There was no way we could put another belt on out on the trail. We talked about our situation for a while and decided to leave the side-by-side there. We called Roger and waited for him to come to get us. While we waited, I suggested that we cover it up with the tarp. As we pulled the tarp over the Arctic Cat, it reminded me of pulling the sheet over the head of a dead person. All hope was lost.

When Roger showed up about an hour later, Shon and I had pretty much written the side-by-side off. It was useless. Roger drove up and asked us what happened. We explained that the belt broke, and it was done. He suggested that we drag it back to the house. I didn't want to see the thing anymore, but Shon decided he might be able to fix it if we got it back to the house where he had more tools. It would be better for it to be at the shop than out in the muskeg anyway. Shon thought it better if we put the Arctic Cat on wheels. We waited for the hour it took for Roger to go to the house and get the wheels. He brought them back in the small, wooden trailer. I was so cold by the time he got back and my mood had NOT improved.

It took about another hour for us to take all four tracks off and put the tires back on. We placed the boards on the muskeg and then used the jack to lift up the side-by-side. We all worked together to get the track off and replace it with a tire. It was a slow process, but we finally got all four tires on.

A plan was quickly hatched by Shon and Roger. I was defeated and cold. I just wanted to be at home. They told me I was going to have to steer the death mobile. Shon would use a crowbar to help make the Argo run, and Roger would drive the Argo. The Argo had some issues of its own and now needed a crowbar placed in just the right place for it to run right. Shon told me to be careful not to let the Arctic Cat run into the back of them when going down a hill. He also told me to try to keep the Arctic Cat on the trail as best as I could. I reluctantly agreed, and we all took our places.

The Arctic Cat was in neutral and followed the Argo with no trouble. We made it through the most challenging part of the trail, and I knew we were going to make it. Roger and Shon pulled me around the back lake, around the corner, and I could finally see our house. About that time, I had a terrible thought. We had to go over a little bridge. Shon and Roger knew that I was terrified of that bridge. I got out every time we drove over it because of the horror I'd witnessed at Cripple Creek. I walked over while Shon drove. He knew I didn't want to drive over it. Surely they would stop and let me out while they pulled the side-by-side over. As we neared the bridge, I had a death grip on the steering wheel. I started hollering for them to stop, but my voice was drowned out by the Argo. I thought about jumping from the moving vehicle but was afraid I would kill us all. Shon and Roger refused to look at me until we were all across that bridge. I was madder than a wet hen. I know I am not supposed to hold grudges, but I will never forget that day.

Sweet Success

After several attempts at moving our belongings from the river to our new home, I had an idea. Each trip was costing us about $500 or more in repairs to the Arctic Cat. And no telling how many years it was taking off of our lives. I sent my grocery list to Walt's wife,

Bonnie, and she got my groceries. Walt was going to deliver them the next day. He and I were discussing the details over the phone when I decided to ask him how much he would charge to our supplies the three miles from the river. It would be just a quick hop over in the airplane. He knew how much trouble we were having and I'm pretty sure he felt sorry for us. He thought it over for a minute and said he would charge $75 a load. That sounded like a deal to me. He asked how many trips I thought we needed. I told him I thought we could at least get the necessities in 5 trips. I did some quick calculations. Even I could tell that $375 was less than $500. He said he would have the necessary fuel onboard the next day to assist in the final push to get us moved. I called Mike and Patti to ask them if we could land on their runway, and they, too, felt sorry for us. Mike gave me his blessing.

I was so excited that next day. We had a plan. When Walt dropped off the groceries, I got into the plane with him. He took me over to Mike and Patti's place, where all of our supplies were under that big shed, so I could pick the supplies that I thought would be the most useful. I had my gun, my cell phone, and a knife to open boxes. When he and I landed, I started making a pile of the most essential items, and he started loading the plane. I was surprised at how much he stuffed in that small airplane. After about fifteen minutes, he took off fully loaded, leaving me to continue sorting through. I was fearful that a bear was going to sneak up on me. I had never been so entirely alone, but I didn't have time to contemplate a grizzly end. I had sorting to do. I had a pretty nice pile set aside when he returned. I was surprised, however, at how quickly he unloaded and returned. I needed to work fast because I knew he didn't want to be waiting around. I stopped sorting to help him load, but he told me he would load the plane if I would just get the next load ready. And he was off once more.

I couldn't believe how fast this was going and how much we were getting into each load. I was having so much fun seeing our stuff. It was like Christmas morning, opening up box after box, finding things I hadn't seen for a couple of months. The belongings were especially precious because they were all I had saved from our previous life. I started pulling out all of the packing material and stuffing the totes completely full. After a couple of loads, I realized that we could possibly get it all.

We got into a rhythm. I went through the totes while he was gone and had a nice pile stacked up when the plane arrived. On each return trip, Walt loaded the aircraft with another collection of precious cargo. Shon, Roger, and Mirai were working on the other end, moving the supplies from the airstrip to the house. Each load was a victory. We had tried so hard to get our supplies from the river. We were finally achieving our original goal of moving to Alaska. It took seven loads, but we got it all done. On the last trip, Walt and I both got into the Maule. There was no room in that airplane for one more thing. When we landed on the strip at Cub Lake, we were completely moved except for three totes full of packing material and several cardboard boxes.

In a couple of weeks, the temperatures dropped down enough that the ground completely froze. We drove to the river with no problems and picked up the last of the totes and trash. I remembered what Mike said about getting our supplies with a pogo stick and finally knew what he meant. A week later, though, there was so much snow that we couldn't drive anywhere. We weren't in Texas anymore. Alaska was more challenging than we could ever have imagined, but we accomplished our first goal. We moved in.

*"For I know the plans I have for you," declares
the Lord, "plans to prosper you and not to harm
you, plans to give you hope and a future."*

Jeremiah 29:11 NIV

CHAPTER 3

Adjusting to Life in the Wilderness

Wood for Winter

When we first got to Cub Lake at the end of August, the fireweed was losing its blooms. They were replaced with puffy white tufts that looked like smoke. Most of the strawberries had come and gone. The leaves on the birch trees had changed colors and started falling, creating a carpet of orange leaves on our beautiful green lawn. It rained every day. It didn't rain hard, but every day there was a slow, steady mist that created puddles on the already saturated ground. Everything was completely soaked. The trails around the cabin were muddy. We frequently found ourselves fighting the Arctic Cat and the tracks that were supposed to be so effective in the bush. I questioned why the thing was called an all-terrain vehicle. Even with all of the challenges, we couldn't quit. Besides needing to get our belongings from the river, we also had to get wood for winter. The cold temperatures reminded us every day that snow was right around the corner.

Nothing struck fear into my heart like not having enough wood for our first Alaskan winter. I knew it weighed on Shon as well. While still in Texas, Shon researched chainsaws and found what we needed to get a good wood supply. We bought what we needed in Anchorage, and the orange Husqvarna was one of the first things Shon retrieved from the river, along with the food and guns. Anytime we weren't trying to get our belongings from the river, we were getting firewood. It helped get my mind off our epic failure of moving, so I was all for it. Our confidence was pretty well shot, so we weren't in the best of moods when we started on this second, even more critical, aspect of living in Alaska.

Mirai wanted to be a part of the firewood adventure. We all put on our rain jackets, gloves, and waterproof boots. We stuffed our mosquito nets in our pockets to use when the rain gave way to the sun. The annoying little critters liked to swarm around our heads while we were working. We got in the side-by-side, praying that it would get us down the trail. It only had two seats, so Mirai and I shared the passenger's side while Shon drove. We drove down trails around our house, looking for any birch tree or standing dead spruce that looked like it might be reasonably easy to get. We didn't know what we were doing. We were *cheechakoes* for sure. (*Cheechako* is a term for a newcomer to Alaska who doesn't have skill or understanding of the wilderness. The opposite of a cheechako is a *sourdough*, someone who knows how to survive and thrive up North.)

Shon cut the trees down, bucked the trees into manageable pieces, and Mirai and I hauled the rounds to the trail. We stacked the wood next to the path after we had as much as we could get into the back of the Arctic Cat. It was difficult getting the wood from the trail to the house without losing a track or getting stuck. We piled all of the rounds near the cabin by the underporch. (The underporch is an area located directly under our front porch. It is at the front of the house and opens up like a garage on the East end. It is where we keep a good supply of firewood, our freezers, animal feed, and our propane tanks. It has a garage door on it to keep the bears out.) When we weren't gathering the wood, we were splitting it. Shon was surprised when I wanted to learn how to cut wood, but I wanted to help as much as possible. It was my turn to be surprised when I saw Mirai pick up my maul and start splitting wood as well. She had listened when Shon taught me. She and I couldn't split the huge rounds, but we could split the small ones or the ones Shon had already halved. We enjoyed seeing the progress we were making as we carried wheelbarrow loads of split firewood into the underporch. The wood was wet from the rain and from being freshly cut, but it was wood.

One day we went out to get another load of wood. We saw a big spruce tree that had fallen and several birch trees that looked promising all in the same little area. Mirai and I waited as Shon cut the spruce tree into rounds. While we were waiting, Mirai stomped all of the ferns down in our work area to make it easier for us to walk. I was impressed! Stomping out a path made it so much easier when it was time for us to carry the heavy rounds back to the trail. We were all feeling pretty good about our work.

We went back to this cleared area the next day, ready to tackle the big birch trees. We were all wearing our ear protection as Shon started up the chainsaw and made his first cut to the tree. He made several cuts, and we knew it was almost time for the tree to come down. It was all going fine until the tree shifted wrong and caught Shon's bar. It didn't matter how hard he pulled the chainsaw or pushed the tree, it was stuck. Instead of falling the opposite direction, the tree had fallen onto his bar. It was standing straight up like it had never been cut. The tree was cut all the way through, it just needed a little help to go the other way. Shon and I decided that we needed to use the now familiar come-along to help us get out of our predicament. We got everything hooked up and started pulling the tree carefully until finally, the tree started its fall in the right direction, freeing the chainsaw. We were happy until the tree fell directly into another birch tree that was forked at the top. The chainsaw was okay, but the birch tree wasn't going anywhere. That birch tree was stuck in the other birch until the next year when Shon finally figured out a way to get it down safely. We now call that trail Forked Tree Lane.

We learned a lot that autumn about getting firewood. Every lesson seemed to come from something we did that could have been disastrous. Our wood was wet, and our process left a lot to be desired. Our biggest takeaway was that we didn't know what the heck we were doing and needed a better way.

Food Storage

One of my favorite things about the cabin at Cub Lake was the pantry. It was huge. I loved getting our food from the river and stocking the shelves. I don't know what is so satisfying about having a fully stocked pantry, but I loved it. We bought five-gallon, food-grade buckets with twist lids and filled them with the basics: flour, sugar, brown sugar, rice, and beans. I also had cases of various canned food. My stash included plenty of peanut butter, olive oil, cooking oil, salt, and spices. I had a good supply of coffee as well. I knew I couldn't just run to the store around the corner as I did in El Paso, so I stocked up on anything I used for cooking. My goal was to have enough staples to last for a year because I knew that trips to town were going to be few and far between.

Getting supplies from Wasilla was tricky. If I went to town to get groceries, it was a trip in and then another trip out. If I got Walt's wife to pick up my groceries, it was just one trip out, saving us quite a bit on the air taxi. Bonnie was kind enough to get groceries for me while we figured out what we were doing. I sent lists to her by text message. She shopped for me when she was going to town to do her shopping, and then Walt brought the groceries out, usually with another part for the Arctic Cat. Because I bought most of my staples in bulk and had them barged out, I only had to replenish the perishables and items that I used faster than I thought I would. It was surprising how quickly I went through yeast, baking powder, and flour. Cooking all of our bread from scratch, I used up these items much quicker than I expected. I had never made our bread and tortillas, so there was a learning curve.

Getting eggs, milk, and meat from town was especially hard. I ended up buying powdered milk and eggs to use in all of my baking. I couldn't tell the difference in the taste, and it was a huge game-changer. I wondered why I hadn't done that before. It saved money, and both were shelf-stable. We still got milk and eggs, but they were never used in baking. We drank the milk or put it in our coffee, but it never went into a recipe. Eggs were scrambled or fried. Powdered eggs were used when I made pancakes or muffins. Getting the meat from town was another challenge. I finally bought a half hog and a quarter beef from a butcher shop to make it easier on Bonnie. After the weather changed and we had continually freezing temperatures, the meat was easy to store in the freezer in the underporch. We didn't even have to plug it in.

My pantry may have been huge, but my refrigerator was tiny. It was a propane fridge about the size of one you might find in an RV. Shon even took the lightbulb out of it to save on electricity, adding insult to injury, if you ask me. How the heck was I to store enough food in that fridge to last four to six weeks? Downstairs, off of the pantry, was the cold storage, but it wasn't too cold when we first got to Cub Lake. It stayed about sixty degrees in the summer and then got closer to thirty-five to forty degrees during the colder months. In the winter, it acts like a big walk-in refrigerator, which was really helpful. The summer months were when I had to adjust. I finally figured out that there were some items that I refrigerated that do fine if they are just cool. For instance, pickles and ketchup are just fine kept in a cool dark place. If I found that my fridge just couldn't hold everything when I got a big load from town, I put the overflow in an ice chest that I kept in the cold storage. I kept the lid closed and would keep the temperature lower by putting frozen meat in the cooler that needed to thaw anyway. As I got better at figuring out my food storage, I quit having to use the ice chest.

I had no idea how much toilet paper or paper towels we would use in a year. Plastic baggies, aluminum foil, cleaning supplies, mouthwash, and toothpaste all had to be brought out. And all of these supplies had to be replenished as economically as possible.

It felt terrific being well-stocked, knowing that water and wild game were also readily available. If nothing else, we were prepared in case of the Apocalypse or a zombie invasion.

Northern Lights and Chocolate Moose

Mirai wanted to see the Northern Lights. I was worried about wood and getting all of our things from the river, but those things

60

didn't seem to bother my sweet daughter-in-law. For several nights, she stayed up until midnight watching the sky. When we got up in the mornings, I would ask her if she'd had any luck. After about a week, she gave up and went to bed when we did.

We all went to bed about ten p.m. one night, about three weeks into our Alaskan adventure. I woke up around two a.m.. I got up and looked outside, hoping to catch a glimpse of the magical light show. I noticed a slight glow on the horizon to the north. I wasn't sure what it was. I went to the living room to look out of the big picture window, where I could see to the northeast. I could observe the light better and noticed small ribbons dancing in the sky. Before waking Shon and Mirai, I wanted to be sure it really was the Northern Lights. I opened the back door, so I could have a better view of the north. As soon as I was outside, I knew this was it. I rushed in, woke Shon up gently, and then quietly called down the stairs to Mirai. She was up in just a second.

Our house was designed to face the south to catch the most sun. We only had two small windows that faced directly north, so to get a good view of the lights, we had to go outside. At first, we all went out in our pajamas. We got cold quickly. In just a few minutes, we all had on jackets, gloves, and house slippers with our faces turned towards the heavens in the north. It was absolutely magical. Ribbons of light sprung up from the horizon, dancing around in the sky, then disappearing into the cold night. The thin strands of light sprung up in several different directions. We found ourselves saying, "*Ooooh,* look at that one!" pointing to an image that quickly disappeared. The show intensified and then almost seemed to fade away.

We stood outside, waiting for the lights to return when we heard a sound in the forest nearby. It scared Mirai and me. We hustled up the stairs to the safety of the back door while Shon laughed at us. He pulled a flashlight from his coat pocket and pointed it towards the crunching sound. Two glowing eyes peered at us through the brush. The area around our house was cleared, but there were trees and brush 100 feet from our back door. The moose was munching on the willows, slowly heading our direction. When she finally came out of the forest, she kept her eyes on us as she walked along the side of the house. I had to talk to her, of course. I said, "Hi, Moose. How's it going?" She stopped and looked at me. I asked Mirai what we should name her. After a moment, Mirai said the moose's name would be Chocolate. Chocolate continued on her way, and the light show returned. We all stood there until we were freezing cold, amazed at the beauty that God created and thankful that we were there to witness it.

Stretch

I didn't know my husband was a mechanic. I appreciated his skills when we started having trouble with our only vehicle. Making trips to the river was causing us all sorts of problems with the Arctic Cat. Shon spent lots of time looking at the side-by-side, and I was quickly forming a strong dislike for the thing.

Mirai and I were stacking wood in the underporch one morning. She brought the wood in from a big pile out in the yard, handed it to me, and I stacked it neatly near the back door. We were working well together, even though we didn't talk much. We were still getting to know each other.

She had her arms full of wood and was heading in when we both heard Shon say, "Help!" It didn't sound bad, so she handed the wood to me, and Mirai went back out to see if she could lend Shon a hand. I stacked the wood and then turned back around when I heard Shon repeat "*Help!*" This time he had some concern in his voice. When I saw Mirai's face, I knew something was terribly wrong. Her eyes were as big as saucers, and she wasn't running to help Shon. She looked at me with a panicked expression, telling me with her eyes that I needed to act fast.

I ran out of the underporch into the yard, where Shon was working on the Arctic Cat. His right foot and leg were under the left back track, and his right foot was inside the Arctic Cat near the gas pedal. He was practically doing the splits. Shon is one of the least limber people I have ever known, so this predicament was disconcerting, to say the least. He broke his right ankle when he was twenty, and there it was, pinned under the big, mean track. All I could think was, "We are a long way from the hospital."

The seat of the driver's side of the Arctic cat was lying on the ground. Shon had removed it to access the battery. He calmly told me to climb over him into the driver's side of the vehicle. When I did, my weight put more pressure on his...well....his predicament. I apologized, but knew I had to continue. He told me to put the vehicle in reverse. I thought we needed to pull forward, but he assured me that was incorrect. I did as he asked. He then told me to carefully step on the gas. I was scared. I knew how that thing worked. It never moved slowly, especially in reverse. It liked to lunge. I didn't want to cause an even bigger problem, so I barely pressed the gas down. It lurched backward a bit, but not enough. Shon felt a bit better but needed it entirely off of his foot. He told me to press it again. I did as he instructed, and he broke free of the weight of the machine.

Mirai was standing there, watching, as Shon started walking around the yard, checking to see if his legs still worked. She looked so relieved...until the fight broke out. I'm not sure why, but after I realized that Shon wasn't hurt, I was furious. What was he thinking? How did Shon get himself into that position? Didn't he know that we were a long way from the hospital? *How did this happen?*

Apparently, Shon was in no mood for my mouth. Shon is usually a tranquil guy, but after just a minute of my butt-chewing, he'd had enough. He started hollering back at me. "You know damn well how this happened." I had to go into the house to get myself together. Shon stomped around the yard, mad at the Arctic Cat and me. Mirai quietly went back to stacking wood. No telling what she was thinking.

Living with Less

We had never lived off-grid before. Our entire lives were lived with plenty of electricity, but we never thought we were wasteful. I knew that my electricity usage had to change when Shon pulled that light out of my fridge. And guess what? I could still find what I needed. It surprises me now when I open someone's refrigerator and it lights up like the Vegas strip. We also changed every light bulb in the house to LED, and we never left the room with a lamp on. Shon would say, "Who do you think you are? Tom Bodett?" I learned quickly to turn the lights off. We also used headlamps, which made us all look like dorks. We went through a lot of candles, as well.

I had to learn what appliances I could use without the generator running. That was easy. I couldn't use any of them except for my mixer. The vacuum, microwave, washing machine, and blender could not be used. The blow drier was out of the question, and I didn't even bring my curling iron. I ended up taking the microwave out of the kitchen and putting it downstairs. It was taking up counter space, and I didn't use it anyway. I could use my sewing machine, but it was marginal. We figured out that I could sew when we had wind from the wind generator to supplement the solar panels. I laughed at myself as I found my thought process changing. Never before had I equated a windy day with a good day to sew. Soon I realized that I needed it to be windy and cold. I couldn't plug in my iron to press seams. I had to put it on the wood stove to heat it up like the old pioneers. There were times when I felt like I couldn't do anything, and Shon felt like the electricity police. It took time for us to adjust and learn to communicate what we needed.

Not only was Shon the electricity monitor, but he also had a tight rein on our propane usage. We only had so much. When we ran out, we would not be able to cook, run the refrigerator, or have hot water. We couldn't do anything to conserve propane with the fridge, except to keep it closed as much as possible. The water heater was proving to be a propane hog, so Shon turned it to "vacation" mode until it was time for showers. He turned it up a few hours before shower time, and it worked sufficiently. That saved quite a bit. The stove is what got me. I couldn't just turn the oven on any time I wanted. It used lots of propane. When I cooked bread, I cooked 4 loaves at a time. I didn't use the oven for cooking a roast. I learned to use the wood stove as my slow cooker. I even figured out how to make biscuits in my Dutch oven on top of the stove. Every time we ran out of a bottle of propane and Shon started a new one, he wrote it on the calendar so we could keep up with our usage. It took both of us working together. Through it all, Mirai adjusted right along with us.

With all of the rain, puddles, and the lake out front, it surprised me that we also had to conserve water. We had a great well, but it took electricity to pump it out of the ground. And the pump needed the generator. It didn't take Mirai and me long to realize that we ran out of water really fast if we tried to wash the dishes after every meal.

We started cleaning up the kitchen in the evenings when Shon had the generator going. That was also when we showered. Mirai found several pitchers and filled them with water one evening and left them on the counter. The next day after breakfast, she used the water from the pitcher to pour over the dirty dishes so they wouldn't be so hard to wash in the evenings. We also used the water from the pitchers to fill the drinking water that we kept in the fridge. It was a great way to have a little more water available during the day without depleting our supply in the water tank.

We thought we were conservative with our supplies before moving to the cabin on Cub Lake, but we took it to a whole other level when we got here. Nothing was thrown away that might be used again. We all had a new appreciation for many of the things that we took for granted before. We were also much more careful about what we chose to haul out here. If it wasn't useful and necessary, it didn't make the cut.

Mirai

The time we had with Mirai in the bush was precious. I slowly got to know her even though she never talked much. Shon said I spoke enough for both of us, which was probably what I needed to do. She brought a box of English vocabulary flashcards. She picked three to five words each day, and I put each one in a sentence. I talked to her about connotations and sayings that might trip her up. After we got our supplies from the river, we played Scrabble every afternoon around three while drinking hot tea. Any word she didn't know, I would tell her the meaning and put it in a sentence. She asked some questions but was still pretty quiet.

We went on lots of walks. Mirai loved looking for animal signs, both tracks and scat. She took her phone and would take pictures of all of it. One morning I was in the kitchen when she came in very excited and said, "I found someone's poop!" She wanted me to go out so she could show me the moose poop that she had discovered. It eventually turned into her routine to go out after breakfast to see if any animals had come close to the house. She investigated each track and would try to figure out what had traveled through our land during the night.

Even though I was doing the majority of the talking out of the three of us, Mirai decided she could talk to Shon. It wasn't a regular conversation, however. It was always something funny. One day as Shon's beard was growing out, she looked at him and exclaimed, "Three colors!" Of course, she just laughed and laughed. It took us a while to realize that she was making fun of his beard, which had three colors to it. It was light brown, dark brown, with lots of grays. If anyone else had pointed it out, he might have been offended. Still, Shon was so proud that his daughter-in-law felt comfortable enough around him to make him the butt of her jokes.

Another day I looked outside and saw an unusual sight. Shon was bent over working on the Arctic Cat, a never-ending ordeal. He didn't even know that Mirai was behind him with a big, bent stick. I watched to see what in the world she was doing. She slung that stick over her shoulder and then threw it out in front of her like she was casting with a fishing pole. She planted her feet like she had caught a big fish and started reeling Shon in. Shon had no clue he was part of this drama, and Mirai didn't know that I was in the house laughing at her charade.

After we had returned from one of our disastrous trips to the river, we got home to find Mirai chasing the chickens around the yard. Our neighbor had given us a few chickens, and we had built a makeshift coop and yard for them. Somehow, two of them had escaped, and it worried Mirai. She spent about two hours trying to catch them. When we finally got home, I was so frazzled from our unsuccessful trip that I was in no mood to deal with rogue chickens. I saw the frustration on her face. I went over to the coop where they were and told her I was going to trap the chicken.

The hen was in a corner next to the shed. Apparently, Mirai had tried this maneuver several times before because she shook her head no and said, "The chicken *knows*." I was tired and hungry. I'd never caught a chicken in my life, but I reached down there and grabbed that chicken. I threw her over the fence before she knew what happened. And lickety-split, I did the same with chicken number two. I was a little surprised at myself, but not as surprised as Mirai. I could tell she was impressed. Little did she know that I just didn't have the strength to mess with those birds. It was all or nothing, and I just lucked out.

Mirai, Ann, and Shon in the canoe on Cub Lake,
September of 2016. Photo Credit: Mirai Parker

I'm not sure I would have made it those first few months without the quiet presence of my sweet daughter-in-law. I doubt she will ever know how much she helped me adjust to my strange new life in Alaska.

I can do all things through Him
who gives me strength.

Philippians 4:13 NIV

CHAPTER 4

Our First Winter

Shon's First Snow Machine Trip

It became fairly evident to us, and fairly soon, that we needed some reliable transportation. It was a pretty sad day for me when I realized that the only vehicle that we owned that didn't get stuck or break down was the canoe. And when the lake froze, that mode of transportation was no longer an option. When we only had our feet to get around, Shon started a quest. We needed transportation for the winter. He decided we needed a snow machine that could haul supplies. Having to hire a charter plane for every bit of our supplies was pricy, and some things just won't fit into a Maule. He began his research. He spent hours and hours looking at various snow machines online until he finally decided on one. Around the middle of November, he had chosen a Skandic Super Wide Track to be our new ride.

After deciding on the Super Wide Track, he started learning how to ride a snow machine. We didn't have one yet and wouldn't be able to get one for another month, but that did not stop him. He got on YouTube and watched every snow machine video he could find. He was convinced that he could fly to town, buy the machine, and ride it the fifty-five miles to our house on the frozen river through the Alaskan wilderness. Before I knew it, he called a snow machine shop and bought one over the phone. I think that was when it hit me that he was really going to do it. We had a GPS, and he had heard that the river was marked with stakes, so he assured me that he would be fine. The more I thought about it, the more I thought he would die a cold, slow death, and I would never be able to recover the body. Shon had never liked the cold much, and I was sure that it was a foreshadowing of his upcoming doom.

Our neighbor, Roger, had made the trip once before. He had been with a friend, and it had been a harrowing ordeal. It was one he didn't want to relive. When he realized that Shon was serious about the trip, he started making some suggestions. He knew there were some stops on the river where Shon could check-in. I surmised that those stops might allow me to narrow down the search for his body. Shon had been a pilot and had flown all over Texas. I knew he was capable, but he had never even been on a snow machine, and he had never seen the river in the winter.

After hearing my concerns, Shon got on the phone to see if the river was passable. He called Yentna Station, which is about eighteen miles downriver from us. The guy he talked to suggested that he travel with a partner because he had heard reports of drum ice. Now let me tell you about Alaskans. They don't get into your business. They don't tell you what to do. If someone suggests something, you better listen because they probably wouldn't be telling you unless it was life or death. When this guy suggested traveling with a friend, it got my husband's attention.

Shon made a few more calls, including one to our trusty old friend, Larry Heater. He told Shon that he needed to talk to a guy named Ken Lee and gave Shon his number. Shon had been on the phone all afternoon trying to plan this trip, but he made one more call.

Ken Lee was more than helpful. He's a talker, so getting information from him was not an issue. Ken had already made three trips that winter to Skwentna hauling fuel. He told him that the river was solid, but there wasn't much snow. After Shon explained where we lived and that he had never been on a snow machine, Ken suggested that Shon get the snow machine delivered to Deshka Landing on the following Saturday. Shon could follow Ken as far as the 20-mile slough, which was where Larry Heater had dropped off our supplies just a few months before. Shon knew the rest of the way home from our many trips trying to get our supplies. Shon readily agreed, and I was relieved. Maybe he wouldn't die on this trip. And if he did, at least Ken would be able to lead someone to the corpse.

Roger and Shon flew to town together on a Friday in the middle of December. Roger had Christmas shopping to do, so they shared an air taxi into town. Shon went into Wasilla and bought a large plastic tub to pull behind the snow machine and as many supplies as it would hold. Shon finalized the purchase of the snow machine over the phone. He also arranged for the delivery man to pick him up at the hotel on his way to deliver our new ride to Deshka Landing.

Deshka Landing is the gateway to the Susitna, Yentna River system. It is almost like a little town. They sell fuel, supplies, services, lodging, food, and more. Larry Heater and his wife lived there. It is gated, but it isn't a fancy neighborhood, it just has a gate that you have to pay to go through. People pay to park there and use the access to the river. A day pass or a season's pass can be purchased, depending on how long you need access. Of course, in the summer there are boats and barges. In the winter there are snow machines. It is a pretty busy place. There is a restaurant outside of the gate called Eaglequest, and Shon was to meet Ken there. Shon got there a little early and ordered some breakfast.

Now, like most little communities, everyone knows everyone else, so people recognized Shon as a stranger immediately. Shon enjoyed listening to the laughter and easy chatter of people who were very comfortable in their surroundings. It didn't take them long to ask Shon what his story was.

Shon is not a big talker and is a pretty private guy (We do live in remote AK), so he gave them the basics. He mentioned that we lived off of the Yentna River, he'd bought a new snow machine, and was meeting a guy who was going to let him follow him up the river. They all got quiet, and someone asked who he was following. Everyone leaned in to hear Shon's answer because this could be pretty interesting. Shon answered, "Ken Lee." The restaurant exploded in laughter. Shon heard several people say, "Good luck keeping up with Ken."

After Shon had his breakfast, he gave me a call and told me what had happened. All of my good feelings about the trip dissolved. I was convinced once again that by day's end, I would be a widow.

After Shon's call, it started snowing. It snowed pretty hard that morning. Mirai and I went out and walked around in our snowshoes, testing them out. We had had a little bit of snow, but this was by far the most snowfall we had experienced since moving to Alaska. We got about a foot of snow during that day. We were trying not to be worried about Shon, and it helped to keep busy. This was also the first time she and I had been out in the Alaskan wilderness all alone. Roger was doing his shopping and wouldn't be back until later that day. We had made it the night before by ourselves, but it was going to be a long day of waiting. We played with the dogs, played Scrabble, and kept ourselves busy until we heard Walt bringing Roger home. He got home around three p.m. By the time he got things unloaded and a fire going, it was beginning to grow dark. By four p.m. in the middle of December in Alaska, nightfall has come.

Mirai had played it cool all day. I would ask her, "Are you worried about Shon?" Her answer was always a simple "No." I decided to make dinner, so Shon would have a warm meal when he finally got home. I was in the kitchen cooking when I noticed that Mirai wasn't sitting in her regular place in the living room. She had chosen a chair facing the window with a view toward the end of the lake where Shon would first appear. We both got quieter as our nervousness grew. I had just gotten dinner finished when Mirai let out a yell. "He's *home!*" She jumped up, and we both ran outside to the front porch to see him ride over the lake to the house. He was tired and hungry, but he was home.

Kuma for Christmas

After living in Alaska for just a few months, Shon decided he wanted a dog. I was glad not to have one. I knew that a dog would be beneficial, especially with bears around, but I really thought we should wait a while, at least until summer. That didn't keep him from looking and dreaming. Every day, he showed Mirai and me pictures of dogs he had found online. They weren't like the dogs in Texas. In Texas, you could get dogs from the pound or from almost any Walmart parking lot for next to nothing. I don't know how many dogs I turned down over the years while living in the Lower Forty-Eight. I couldn't imagine having to pay big money for a canine companion! He researched the breeds to find what would work the best out in the bush. He finally decided that we needed a German Shepherd. He asked Mirai to come up with the right name. She settled on Kuma, which means *bear* in Japanese. Shon had the breed, and he now had the name—he just needed the dog. I held my ground. When he changed his research from dogs to snow machines, I thought I'd won this battle.

Little did I know, but Mirai had picked up the search for the perfect Alaskan bush dog. Never think that someone quiet isn't up to something. She talked to Kyle every day while he was stationed overseas. Much of their conversation between October and December revolved around finding a dog for Shon. They had even gotten Jared in on the plot.

One day as I was cleaning up the kitchen, Mirai came in, sat down on a barstool, and announced, "I need to talk to someone." Well, I was super excited about this. I had to work and work to get Mirai to talk to me, so this was thrilling. My thrill turned to chill when I heard her next words: "We are buying a dog for Shon for Christmas!" I absolutely could not hurt her feelings, so I gritted my teeth and replied, "That is a great idea." She was smiling from ear to ear. She quickly opened her tablet and showed me the cutest little German Shepherd puppy she had found on Craigslist. He was adorable. She, Kyle, and Jared had it all worked out. When Kyle and Jared flew in for Christmas, they would pick the puppy and all the needed supplies in Wasilla before flying out to the cabin. It was settled. I'd lost that fight.

I knew how hard it was just getting regular supplies out by plane in the bush. How were those boys going to get a dog out here? I was also worried about money. I knew how much those dogs cost online. Mirai assured me that the dog was already paid for but would not tell me how much they paid. The lady who owned the puppy would keep him another month until the boys were coming in December. The puppy was born in September, and he was the last one of the litter left, so they got a good deal on him. It would work. I tried to not let Mirai see my concerns, but she said they had it under control. I didn't need to worry about a thing.

From time to time, Shon would mention that we needed a dog, trying to get me to change my position on the matter or just giving me a hard time about it, and Mirai would just smile. I continued to tell him that it was a terrible idea getting a puppy in the winter, meaning every word of it. It was a secret that Mirai and I shared. Every once in a while, she would show me the picture of that little puppy, and I was doing my best to get a better attitude about him. It made my heart happy to see Mirai so excited about her surprise for Shon. And I loved that she wanted him to be delighted. She was also missing Kyle and her family in Japan, but this Christmas surprise kept her spirits up.

Mirai started a countdown in the middle of November. I am not sure if it was a countdown to see her husband, Kyle, or the new puppy, Kuma. Either way, we counted each day down with anticipation of the upcoming visit and surprise. We discussed what the boys needed to bring out with the dog. She even got our neighbor, Roger, to get dog food when he went to town. That was going to be his part of the Christmas surprise. She told me she had it all worked out. She informed Kyle and Jared where they needed to sit on the plane and where to have the puppy. She told them how she wanted them to get out of the plane on their arrival, and she was going to get it all on video. She couldn't wait to see Shon's face.

The day finally arrived. We were so excited about the boys getting here, and of course, the added excitement of this adorable little puppy. Mirai and I talked to the boys during the day as they made their way from Anchorage to Wasilla. Our air taxi pilot, Walt, picked them up at Walmart after they did some shopping, took them to the house where Kuma was, and they finally picked him up, after months of planning. He was living with a family who had ten kids. He didn't seem to mind leaving, and the boys had no trouble getting him in the small bush plane after they drove to Willow. He remained pretty calm during the twenty-five-minute flight out to our house.

When the plane finally landed on the frozen lake and the boys got out with Kuma, Shon started hugging the boys and didn't even notice the dog. I did. He was huge! He was already about forty or fifty pounds, and he was all paws and ears. I could tell immediately that he had a LOT more growing to do. When it finally hit Shon that his boys and daughter-in-law had gone to great lengths to bring him this dog, he was truly honored. The boys, Mirai, and I all laughed at the little puppy we thought we were getting. That picture was from September. It hadn't occurred to any of us how much he would grow. This was going to be a big dog.

We enjoyed our time with the kids during the time they were in Alaska for the holidays. They were here for a little over a week, so we had a full house. We weren't sure where Kuma fit. I planned on putting him in a tote at night with a blanket, but that was before I realized that this puppy weighed more than any dog I had ever owned. We put a quilt down behind the couch, and he seemed to realize that was his bed. Even after all of the careful planning, we forgot to get any toys for him, so I got busy and made him some chew toys out of some denim I had. He also tried to eat the table legs, the log railings, and the rocking chair. "*No, Kuma!*" was heard quite often during our first Christmas in Alaska. His favorite chew toy was Mirai's slippers....while they were on her feet. I thought he was going to drive me crazy. I was intimidated, and he was huge and had big teeth. He would come after Mirai and me the most. It took me a while to figure out that the mom at his last home took care of him. I think she was so busy with ten kids that he had to be pretty aggressive to get her attention. He had to be trained to act differently.

Kuma's First Meal at the Cabin on Cub Lake

Family Christmas Photo 2016

It was a sad day when Mirai left with Kyle and Jared. Mirai went to Japan to spend time with her family during the last part of Kyle's deployment, so it was just Shon, me, and now Kuma. By the time they all left, I was not very happy about the dog. He scared me, and I wasn't sure what to do with him. I started looking up how to train a German Shepherd. One of the things I found was to get over the dog while they are on the ground to show dominance. I decided that I had to take some of my power back. I was tired of being scared in my own home.

Kuma and Ann became friends

I got over Kuma in the mornings and gave him a belly rub while telling him that I was the boss. I finally got where I could say to him, "Kuma, do you want a belly rub?" and he would lay down. He had lots of energy, so we got a tennis ball and started playing with him. It finally evolved into a "monkey in the middle" game with Kuma being the monkey and Shon and I on either end. We would roll the tennis ball back and forth, and he would try to catch it. It was fun, and I was beginning to enjoy him, but I was still scared of those teeth. There were times that my hand, the tennis ball, and his teeth were closer together than was comfortable. We started throwing the tennis ball over his head to keep our hands safer. It didn't take long to see that he was really a gentle dog. If he was aggressive, it was only because he needed something. I put bells on the front and back doors and taught him to ring the bell if he wanted out. I got his eating habits figured out as well, so the aggression slowly went away as we learned how to deal with each other. Even though he was a gift for Shon, he was quickly becoming my dog, and I had a new best friend.

Let's Go!

Everything was frozen. The snow had fallen, and we had a new snow machine. Shon had made the trip from Deshka Landing and wanted to take me to the river to show me what it was like. I had seen the slough in the summer and late fall but had never seen the main part of the Yentna River. Shon's description of the frozen river piqued my curiosity. I still had flashbacks of all of our failed attempts of moving, so I was hesitant to go down that trail again. My desire to see the frozen river won out, and I jumped on the back of the snow machine. The soggy swamp that I thought was for sure going to kill us had turned into a beautiful winter wonderland. We took a pair of garden shears and cut back the willows on the seismic trail that had slapped us on our trips to get our belongings. I wasn't even scared on the bridge over Cripple Creek. It was frozen over with a nice layer of snow, and we drove over it without a thought. When we got to the slough where Larry Heater had left our belongings, I was surprised to see that the water level had dropped significantly. Shon nosed the snow machine over the hill and down we went into the frozen slough. I held on as we wound around until we finally broke out onto the river.

The river was huge. What surprised me the most, though, were the number of cabins that I saw along the river's edge. Many of them were run down, and it was obvious no one lived in the structures full-time, but it was a sign of civilization that I hadn't seen in a while. While we sat on the river and I took in the beauty, another snow machine came around the corner. I was so excited about seeing another person! He stopped and we visited a few minutes. He lived on our side of the river full-time. He was just three miles from us as the crow flies. He told us that he had heard that we had moved into the cabin at Cub Lake. He had also heard that all of our belongings had been sitting at Mike and Patti's place for all of that time and congratulated us on finally getting moved. We were surprised, and a little embarrassed, that he knew so much about us.

On the trip home, I thought about meeting our neighbor. If he knew that our belongings were sitting at Mike and Patti's for a couple of months, other people probably knew as well. I hated for people to know what idiots we had been about moving. Still, he seemed to be genuinely happy to meet us and didn't hold our lack of knowledge about Alaska against us. When we got home, we started planning our next adventure. We were going to the Skwentna Roadhouse to get a pizza.

Skwentna, Alaska

Skwentna, Alaska, is our closest town. I'm not even sure one would call it a town. They have a post office, a roadhouse, and a dump station where people can take some of their trash. They also have a nice runway and have been the first stop for the Iron Dog, a 2,000-mile snow machine race, for many years. The population currently is thirty-seven, and I haven't met all of them yet.

Our first trip to "town" was memorable. I thought I was going to freeze to death. I rode on the back of the snow machine while Shon drove. He offered to let me drive, but I was intimidated by the new machine and was worried that I would ruin it or kill us both. I wore several layers under my ski suit. I put on my warmest boots with two pairs of socks and donned my best ski gloves. I was cold by the time we got to the river, but since Shon seemed to be doing okay, I decided it was best if I kept my grumbling to myself. Roger was riding along with us on his snow machine and seemed to be doing fine as well. I was a wimp and needed to toughen up.

When we turned onto the river, the temperature dropped, and our speed picked up, causing my hands to get even colder. With each mile, my hands and feet got colder and colder. I tried to take my mind off of my cold extremities by looking for the huge eagles' nests that were in the cottonwood trees along the river. After just a few minutes, the windscreen of my helmet fogged up so I couldn't even see the beautiful surroundings. The trail was rough in places, jarring me at the rear of the machine as we took dips and drove up steep banks. As much as I was trying to enjoy this new experience, I was miserable. I knew that Skwentna was about twenty miles by trail from our house, so I decided to estimate how far we had traveled.

When we finally stopped, I got off of the machine and started walking, trying to warm up. I was frustrated to realize that we had only stopped for Shon and Roger to discuss where we might be. I climbed back on, with them reassuring me that we were almost there.

A few more miles down the road, we stopped again. We were lost. I was almost to the point of tears but thought that they might freeze my face, so I held them back. I jumped off of the machine and started walking again, trying to get some warmth to my feet while Shon and Roger talked about how they must have missed a turn. My feet felt like frozen blocks on the ends of my legs. They called me back when they figured out where we needed to go. I climbed back on, knowing that I couldn't make it back to the house without getting warm first. In just a few more minutes, we were headed down a trail that promised good food and a friendly fire.

Walking into a place of business out in the middle of nowhere was surreal at first. The owner, Cindi, sat down and visited with us as our pizza was in cooking in the oven. I stood by the woodstove with my boots and gloves off with that painful tingling sensation that comes after getting too cold. Cindi was full of useful information. I asked her how she got enough food out to run a business. She explained that most of her groceries were flown out by plane and hauled from the small airport just a few miles away. She did mention that Ken Lee also did some freighting for her when he brought out her fuel by snow machine. We knew Ken from Shon's first snow machine trip out, and I just discovered a new way to get supplies. She also told us that she knew Bob and Ruth, the people who had built our place. I had wondered about them so much and asked her if she was still in contact with them. She was and agreed to pass on our telephone number. The pizza was delicious, and talking to a woman who was surviving this life did wonders for me.

I thought I could make it back home on the back of the snow machine, but when Shon and Roger stopped about halfway home, I finally asked Shon how he was dealing with the cold. He said he wasn't cold at all. The handlebars were heated, and his feet were tucked up behind the front of the machine. He had been warm and cozy the entire trip. He insisted that I drive, and he would ride behind me so I could get warm. I was cold enough to try anything, even driving this new machine, if it meant I might be able to warm up a bit. My hands warmed up immediately, and my feet quickly followed. I did fine until we got to the steep incline in the slough. There was no way I could drive up that bank. I stopped so we could trade back. While stopped, Shon said, "My hands and feet are freezing! I can't believe you made that entire trip without telling me you were cold. From here on out, we have to take turns." He drove us up the incline and down the trail a few feet before stopping so I could drive us the rest of the way home. I had to get over my fear of driving the snow machine if I wanted to go get another pizza and visit with my new friend, Cindi.

Delayed Gratification

Getting supplies was our biggest challenge of living off the road system. Hauling everything in by plane was expensive, and we were continually looking for another way. We called Ken Lee and asked about his freighting business and immediately knew we had hit the jackpot. Ken agreed to pick up anything we needed in town and would freight it out to us for a reasonable fee. I started placing orders at a big box store in Anchorage. Ken or his wife picked up my order, and then he hauled it out on the weekends. He was making runs to the Skwentna Roadhouse with fuel anyway, so he called us on his satellite phone when he got close to the Twenty-Mile Slough. It was fun hopping on the machine, riding down the now-familiar trail, and picking up loads of supplies. We enjoyed visiting with Ken as we transferred the load from his freight sled to our little plastic tub that we hauled behind our machine. I tried to get in as many questions as I could during our short visits. That winter, Ken freighted out our diesel, our propane, groceries, a mattress, and some new solar panels. He was a great source of information and was fun to be around. He taught me how to call a moose, and he quickly became one of my favorite Alaskans.

Another way of getting supplies was through the small post office in Skwentna. On our second trip to Skwentna, we got a post office box. The postmaster, Steve, said that we could have anything delivered to the post office by either using our box number or the physical address of the post office. We started buying supplies online while we had access to the post office by snow machine. It took several weeks for the packages to arrive. They were shipped to Anchorage and then would fly out to Skwentna on Tuesdays and Thursdays, weather permitting. We often saw the mail plane fly right over our house on those days, and I wished they could just throw out our packages. The mail plane only brought what it could hold, so some of our packages sat in Anchorage a while until they could fit.

On weekends we met Ken on the river. During the week, we drove to Skwentna for pizza and a trip to the post office. On one trip, I was driving the snow machine as we turned off of the Yentna River onto the Skwentna River and saw what looked like a large dog ahead. As I drove closer to it, Shon and I realized that it was a wolf. He got his pistol out and started yelling for me to drive faster. I didn't want to drive more quickly. I didn't want to get closer to a wolf. I sped up a little because Shon was hollering so much, but my heart wasn't in it. He was so frustrated at me when the wolf passed in front of us and disappeared into the forest. I can't say that I was disappointed at all.

Just like our visits with Ken, I found that Steve, the postmaster, knew a thing or two about getting things done in Alaska. As Shon loaded up all of our goodies in our plastic tub, I asked questions. I enquired about gardening, getting supplies, gathering wood, and anything else I could think of to ask. Out of all of our conversations, the ones we had about cutting firewood proved to be the most beneficial. He was very patient with all of my questions but never offered any suggestions unless I asked specifically about a topic. Alaskans, especially the ones who lived out here, were fiercely independent but willing to help a neighbor in need. He obviously recognized my need for information.

Steve, Skwentna Postmaster, 2017

Skwentna Post Office

On one trip back from Skwentna, Shon and I were feeling pretty good about our new and improved method of transportation. We were scooting down the trail, taking turns driving, happy to have a nice load from the post office when we realized that we had lost our tub. We turned around and drove several miles looking for our lost bounty. I had just about decided that someone had come along and found it when we saw it sitting in the middle of the river. It almost looked like it was laughing at us. About the time we thought we had something down, we found a new way to screw it up.

Backup

Our confidence was growing. We were getting supplies each week and meeting new people. After each passing day, we were getting a bit braver. Ken told us about an overland trail that wasn't too far from our house. He informed us that it was a trail used when the river started going out. He suggested that it might be a good idea if we could make a trail to it so we could have access to Skwentna when things started melting on the river. It might also help him get supplies to us a little bit longer. Shon and I decided one day, after the long trip to Skwentna, to go see if we could find it. We were tired but felt good, and we were hopeful that we could find the trail to the south of us. He assured us that we would know it when we found it because it was well-traveled and was marked.

We set off from the house that afternoon with me riding on the back. Shon had our GPS and was using it to make sure we were headed in the right direction. We got off of our regular trail and were in deep snow. Shon's machine did an excellent job of breaking the trail, but it was slow going. We were off of our now-familiar path a few miles when he stopped to look at the GPS. He shut off the snow machine as he studied the GPS and surrounding woods. As soon as he shut off our ride in that deep snow, I had a sinking feeling. I was already tired. If the snow machine wouldn't start, I knew I couldn't walk back through the deep snow to the house before dark. I didn't want to say anything, afraid that I might jinx us if I even mentioned the deadly situation we could be facing. Shon stopped looking at the GPS and said, "I think we need to call it a day. Let's do this later." I agreed. I breathed a sigh of relief when the snow machine started without hesitation, and we made the turn back towards home.

That evening, when we were taking off all of our snow gear back at the house, Shon said, "We need another snow machine. What we did today could have gone really bad. We never need to go anywhere without a backup snow machine." I was in complete agreement. We had our second snow machine within a couple of weeks.

Our Snow Machines

Racquetball in the Bush

After I had my snow machine, I really looked forward to our trips to Skwentna to pick up mail. I had gotten to be friends with Bonnie, the postmaster's wife. On one of our package runs, I was quizzing Bonnie about what would grow well in an Alaskan garden when a nice looking gentlemen came in the small log post office. I hated to be interrupted because I was getting valuable information. Still, Bonnie stopped talking to me to get this guy's mail. After they talked a bit, she asked me if I had met Tom. She introduced us, telling Tom that we had moved into the cabin at Cub Lake. The first thing that caught my attention was his mustache. He didn't have a full beard like many Alaskan men, but he had a full mustache and an easy-going grin.

Bonnie told me that Tom had written a book that I might like. He threw in that he had a story in his book about Ruth catching a fish off of our dock that I might want to read. She also said he had the most beautiful lodge around and added that he even had a racquetball court. Well, that caught my attention! Who cares about gardening when there is a racquetball court? I'm sure my eyes lit up when I started telling him that racquetball was my very favorite sport in the whole entire world. (I'm not very subtle.) Little did I know it at the time, but he was just as excited to find someone out in the bush who liked to play racquetball, even though he was much calmer about it. He got my telephone number, and I got his. We agreed that Shon and I would come over sometime to play.

Tom took off with his mail about the time Shon was finished loading our tub with packages. Shon was stunned when I told him about this great opportunity to play racquetball. On the trip home, I got to thinking that it was probably one of those invitations that people throw out but don't really mean. I had to tell myself that I would probably not really get to play my favorite game out in the bush. I had sold all of my equipment in the estate sale, and I didn't even have a good pair of court shoes. And I also got to thinking about what a racquetball court might actually look like in the bush. I started picturing an old barn with a dirt floor. There had to be some kind of heat source, right? Or did these Alaskans play in their winter gear at subzero temperatures? By the time we got home, I had decided that I probably didn't want to play bush racquetball.

The next day, Tom texted me. He asked when Shon and I were coming over. I couldn't really turn the guy down, since I'd been so eager, so I called him and he gave me directions to his house. We were going to play the next day at around ten a.m. He inquired about our shoes. He said that if they made black marks on his court, we could use some of his. Well, at least I knew that it wasn't a dirt floor. I couldn't bring myself to ask if the court was heated.

Tom and Miss Patty at Bentalit Lodge. Check out Tom's book,
Stories I've Heard, Characters I've Met & Lies We've Told
in My 44 Alaskan Years.

Bentalit Lodge

The next morning, Shon and I got on our snow machines around
nine, in the dark, and started towards the river. It took us almost an
hour to find his place. When we came around the corner and saw his

lodge, all of my fears dissolved. This wasn't going to be a converted barn. This was one of the most beautiful lodges I have ever seen. It was majestic. We parked in the back where he had told us to and went in to find not only the best racquetball court, but two of the most delightful people. Tom and his wife, Miss Patty, made us feel right at home.

I quickly realized that Tom loved racquetball even more than I did. That seventy-five-year-old man beat us like a drum without even breaking a sweat. This trip was just the first of lots of early-morning snow machine trips. Tom also had a neighbor named Roger. They played almost every other day at seven a.m. Tom encouraged us to come over as much as possible, which turned out to be about once a week, to play doubles. Shon and Roger partnered up, and Tom and I became partners. He dubbed the two of us "the ol' geezer and the gal" team. Miss Patty was always busy while we were playing but had coffee ready for us when we were through and would come sit with us for the "bull session." Miss Patty was a quiet presence, whereas Tom enjoyed telling stories, some true and some very questionable.

I don't think I could ever tell Tom, and men don't seem to know what to do with it if they are told, but he means the world to me. He helped me survive my first winter in Alaska! And he has continued to help us when we weren't sure what we should do about the different situations that we have faced. His advice has always been sound and comes with a gracious grin under that big mustache.

Bob and Ruth

From the moment I first saw the cabin at Cub Lake, I wondered about the people who had built it. The house was fully furnished, so it felt like we had stepped into someone else's life. When Cindi from the roadhouse in Skwentna gave our phone number to Bob and Ruth, we got a call right away. They were so excited to learn that the home that they had built was finally being enjoyed by another couple. During that first conversation and several more that followed, we enjoyed hearing about the history of the cabin at Cub Lake.

Ruth and Bob

Bob found the small lake with a beautiful piece of land next to it in 1984 and filed on the property. He named it Cub Lake because he flew in and out in his Super Cub. In 1985, he built the guest cabin next to the lake for him and his wife to enjoy. They used it as a weekend getaway with friends, having cookouts and campfires. They had so much fun at Cub Lake that Bob decided to build a home there.

Bob started the process by hauling out the D3 Dozer in the winter of 1986. That is a story in itself that Bob said took ten years off of his life. He used the Dozer to clear the property and started the foundation that summer. He had an Otter, a bush plane, fly out twenty-two loads of lumber and supplies over the next couple of winters. They unloaded on the frozen lake and hauled the load up the hill with snow machines. They covered all of the lumber and supplies with tarps until the summer, when they resumed construction. Bob, Ruth, and several friends worked on the cabin from 1986 until 1993, using plans that Bob had drawn out on his kitchen table.

Bob and Ruth moved to the cabin full time in 1993 and lived in it until 2009. They added the shop in 1998 and 1999. Ruth called that time their "glory years." They sold it to another couple in 2009, but that man and woman never did anything with it. Rumor has it that, when it got time to move from the Lower Forty-Eight, the wife changed her mind about living in the Alaskan wilderness, much to her husband's surprise and disappointment. The cabin sat empty until we bought it in 2016. Bob and Ruth were worried that it would deteriorate with no one caring for it. We had many questions for them, and they had lots of questions for us. We talked to them for a couple of hours during that first conversation. I wrote notes while Shon visited with Bob. They spoke so long that we had to hang up before Ruth and I even got to talk.

Over the years, we have talked with Bob and Ruth numerous times over the phone. We have also visited them at their new home in Arizona. Having this relationship with the precious couple who built the cabin at Cub Lake has indeed been a blessing. Ruth likes to say that she and I are living parallel lives. We enjoy sharing stories about their history and our current life in this wild place that we both love so much.

I wait for the LORD, my whole being waits,
and in his word I put my hope.

Psalm 130:5 NIV

CHAPTER 5

Land of the Midnight Sun

Kuma in the Lake

Living in Texas, we never had four seasons. When we moved to Alaska, one of my favorite things was watching the landscape change entirely from season to season. After seeing white snow from October until April or May, it was thrilling to see the first signs of green in the spring, which Alaskans out in the bush usually refer to as "breakup." During this time, the rivers and lakes begin to thaw, and the ice breaks up, revealing the frigid waters below. Everything slows down because our frozen highways become impassable, and the runway on the lake proves to be unusable. Traveling for us stopped until the ice melted and the winter wonderland was transformed into green splendor.

We watched the lake as the ice gave way in places. The east end was almost entirely free of ice, but our runway and snow machine tracks were holding on. Kuma walked across the lake on the frozen areas but had to pick his way carefully. We lost ice each day because of the warmer temperatures. We watched as he picked his way across, concerned that he might break through the ice, but he seemed to sense the safest route.

After traveling so much by snow machine, it was difficult for me to be in this holding pattern. I was ready to go. One morning, after watching Kuma traverse the lake, I decided I could pull my canoe over to the east end and paddle around the open area. I hadn't been in the boat in several months and had missed it. The snow had thawed entirely on the lawn, so it was reasonably easy to pull the canoe across the green grass. I grabbed my paddle, put on my lifejacket, and pushed off into the freezing water. Kuma was there, as always, wanting to be right by my side. I thought he would run along the bank, which was his custom in the summer, but he decided he could get closer to me on the ice in the middle of the lake. I wasn't too concerned, because he ran across that ice daily. However, this time, he ran along the edge of the ice to be near me. When he was almost to the middle of the lake, the ice broke through. Kuma plunged into the icy water. I screamed for help, and Shon came running from the shop.

It didn't take him long to see what was going on. Kuma was doing his very best to get himself back on to the ice. Shon ran back to get a rope while I paddled quickly towards shore. I watched as Kuma worked to get a foothold on the ice. It broke through several times until he finally got to a piece that was strong enough to hold his weight. As Shon was running back with the rope, Kuma kicked his way back up onto the ice and trotted over to us on the bank. He shook the icy water from his thick coat as if nothing had happened. From then on, I didn't get the canoe out until Kuma was through walking across the lake. And it was another reminder of how quickly things can go wrong in this rugged place we call home.

Greenhouse

One great thing about summer in Alaska is the sun. We have to deal with darkness in the winter, but the summer is glorious. There are times that we deal with dreary rainy days, but most days are full of sunshine. And the sun never sets. It gets dusky around midnight, but never completely dark. As our first summer approached, we had a list of projects that needed to be completed while the snow was gone. The long days gave us plenty of daylight to build several structures.

Our first construction project had to be the greenhouse. Our kitchen table was full of plants that needed a new home. I wanted to make a container garden in the greenhouse using the totes that we mailed from Texas. I took ten empty totes out to the front yard, near the garden area, and laid them out how I wanted them. Shon brought a tape measure, and we moved them around until we were both happy with the dimensions and the location. We were just a few feet from the plot that had been used as a garden by Bob and Ruth. We were also only about fifty feet from the lake. I wanted it to be close, so I could haul lake water for my plants.

We brought in lots of spruce poles during the winter for our construction projects, so we were ready to begin the next morning. Shon took a shovel and started digging a hole where he wanted to sink the first pole. It didn't take him long to get down a couple of feet. Unlike Texas, it was easy digging, but it also filled up with water. Construction in the bush was already proving to be different than what we had anticipated. Instead of sinking the posts, we had to make a rectangular base on the ground out of four poles. We then build up from that. The change in plans made a bit more work for us, but it also allowed the greenhouse to be moved if we ever decided it needed to go to another location. Working with round logs instead of rectangular 2x4's was tricky. It took us about a week to complete the frame, and then we covered the bottom half with chicken wire. After adding the additional support for the walls, we covered it completely with clear plastic. I'd found an old, homemade door in a pile of junk and had pulled it out. I stapled chicken wire to the frame and then covered it with clear plastic as well. After we got the door on the structure, we stood back and admired our handiwork. Playing with Lincoln Logs as kids had really paid off.

Our Greenhouse, Summer 2017

Gardening

I had a huge garden when we were in Texas and considered myself a decent gardener. I grew tomatoes and jalapenos without even having to try. My Texas gardening skills didn't transfer well to

Ann was excited about her first Alaskan cabbage, Summer 2017

Alaska. I'd never started my garden plants from seeds before, but I knew I couldn't take a trip to town just for starts. I bought seeds at the end of the last summer, along with trays with lids that would act as a terrarium. I tried to figure out when to start the seeds so they would be ready to transplant by the first of June. That was a bit tricky, but I did my best. Many of the plants were "leggy" by the time we had the greenhouse up. I filled the totes with the soil we dug up near the chicken coop mixed with garden soil I bought from town. I had saved my eggshells all winter, dried them, crushed them, and mixed them in to help bring the acidity of the soil down. I put the tomatoes and jalapenos in the greenhouse, along with bell peppers and cucumbers. We tilled the garden, and I carefully planted squash, cabbage, and okra. I was so excited about the garden. It was lots of hard work, and I was looking forward to my bounty. I'm embarrassed to say that the only thing I got out of that first garden was cabbage. And we don't even like cabbage that much. Over the years, I have become a better Alaskan gardener, but don't expect to see one of my zucchinis at the

Alaska State Fair. If I grow one out in the bush, we are eating it. I'm sure as heck not hauling it to town.

Stowaway

I love my canoe. I enjoy getting out in the early morning when the lake is still to take a quiet ride all by myself. On one such morning, Kuma ran along the bank to make sure I wasn't in any danger. It was a time for me to let my mind clear, and my feelings get sorted out. I enjoyed having time to pray about things that were bothering me and let God speak to my heart in His still, small voice.

It was a beautiful summer morning. I went out in the fresh, brisk air with my life jacket in one hand and a paddle in the other. I was wearing my typical bush attire....cap, head net, long sleeve shirt, jeans, muck boots, and a .45 pistol on my hip for bears. I enjoyed the short walk from the house to the lake, taking in the gorgeous wildflowers and the swallows swooping down, catching mosquitoes. The canoe was up on the bank, turned over to keep the rain out. I flipped it over and maneuvered it in the lake. We had been getting quite a bit of rain, so I couldn't just leave it in the slip, or it would fill with water. Kuma was excited that we were going on an adventure and wagged his tail while I got settled into the canoe. I used my paddle to push off of the land. When I was clear of the slip, I nosed the boat toward the inlet. I was just beginning to talk to God as I was nearing the west bank when a small gray mouse poked his head out of the opposite end of the canoe. He must have found a comfortable dry place to get out of the rain during the night. He was as surprised to see me as I was to see him.

I just have to say, I don't like mice. They are repulsive. They creep me out. I don't like their eyes or their whiskers, and I abhor how they scurry about. I started telling this mouse that he needed to stay on his end of the canoe. I assured the nasty rodent that I would stay on my end, all while getting that boat turned around so I could get back to the land. The mouse acted like he was listening, but apparently, he didn't quite understand. He started down the length of the canoe straight at me. I started beating the bottom of the boat with my paddle, trying to scare him back. He just dodged the paddle and ran right between my legs, under my seat. I was screaming at this point because my paddle was of no use, and I was having trouble keeping my eye on the little devil. I was convinced that he was going to run right up one of my muck boots into my lap.

My screaming seemed to help, because he ran back to his end of the canoe, turned, and looked at me. I was paddling like crazy now, trying to get to the slip so I could escape the infested boat. I thought that the mouse and I had an understanding when he slipped back into the small compartment that was his original hiding place. I was paddling like nobody's business.

Kuma realized that I was in distress and started barking his head off on the bank, trying to get to me. I was headed home when that ugly little rodent came back out. I almost felt sorry for him. He was shaking all over. I told him again that he needed to stay there. Clearly, he must not have understood, because he took another run at me. Again, I tried to encourage a retreat with my paddle, but I didn't make any contact, and he was dead set on sharing my end of the canoe. Thankfully, I forgot about the gun on my hip, or my reliable canoe would be full of holes. He disappeared into the compartment at my end of the canoe. I finally made it to the bank, exhausted, terrified, and feeling a little sheepish when I saw Shon there, ready to defend me from a bear. I hated to tell him that all of the hysterics were due to a mouse. Then again, how many women have to endure sharing a canoe with a stowaway mouse? We pulled the boat out of the water and turned it over. I beat on the thing with my paddle, trying to get rid of my new little enemy. He scurried away while Shon chuckled at my displeasure. I vowed then and there to always give any mice an eviction notice before setting off in the canoe to experience my quiet time. Peaceful reflection in my canoe just wasn't the same when there was a mouse on board.

Lazarus

I had a flock of twelve chickens I got from town. Why twelve, you might ask? Well, you buy eggs by the dozen, and we were looking for eggs, so it only seemed logical to buy twelve hens. I got the chickens from a guy in Wasilla on one of our frantic supply trips to town. We had to get the chicks last and then head straight to the plane. He lived farther out than expected, so we didn't have much time to ask questions. He was pushing his Naked Necks, which he said would be great for Alaska weather. I wanted a mixture of breeds so I could see what worked best for us. He guaranteed that they would all be hens, and if they weren't, we could return the roos. That was easier said than done for us, so we knew we were taking a chance. I ended up grabbing three Naked Necks, five Rhode Island Reds, two Austrolorps, and two Plymouth Rocks. They were about two to three days old, and all fit in a shoebox with plenty of room to spare. They sat on my lap on the plane ride out, chirping up a storm.

When we got home, we fixed up a dog kennel for them. I put small cardboard boxes on their sides so they would have places to huddle together. Because of our electricity situation, we couldn't run a powerful heat lamp. We rigged up a single bulb, and I put hot water in bottles to help keep them warm. Every morning I would check on them, pleased to find all twelve healthy. It was entertaining to change up the cardboard boxes, making various homes for them. I used willow branches to give them small perches. Every once in a while, one would escape the kennel, but I always seemed to notice before Kuma did, thankfully. He seemed to enjoy watching them almost as much as I did. They grew louder and messier each day, which was a good motivator for us to get the chicken coop finished. With the completion of the chicken coop, we moved the dirty little dozen outside after a few weeks. I had my suspicions that they weren't all hens about the time we were moving them out. One seemed to be the leader, and there were a couple of more that were just a little bigger than the rest. Every morning I would rush out to see if they were all still among the living. Somehow, they all made it to adulthood.

All in all, I ended up with nine hens. The three roosters were all different breeds. The most dominant roo was the Rhode Island Red I ended up giving to Roger, our neighbor across the lake. Next in line was the beautiful black and white Plymouth Rock, who seemed pretty mellow. The last in the pecking order was a Naked Neck. Shon and I had about decided that I had gotten a pretty raw deal on the Naked Necks. Who wanted chickens in Alaska that didn't have feathers on their necks? We had enough trouble with frostbite on their feet and heads. What in the world would I do to protect their necks? I had friends who suggested I knit them little scarves, but that always ended with a bit of a snicker. What was I thinking? I ended up giving the three naked necks, including the rooster, to some neighbors who needed the food. It was sad when they carried them away for slaughter. I was especially sorry about the one I had named Daisy, who had become my favorite from day one. So I was down to eight: seven hens and the beautiful black-and-white rooster that was getting more majestic every day.

We had some neighbors move into a cabin not far from us for a short time. They had four kids, ranging in ages eighteen months to eleven years. The kids came over and asked if they could see my chickens. We had been training Kuma to leave the chickens alone. When he would get too close, we would tell him *no*. He wanted to play with them in the worst way. They ran around, flapped their wings, and even seemed to have a squeaker. They were the perfect dog toy. It never occurred to me that the children might need some training as well. When I took the four kids down to the chicken coop, they started running around, trying to catch my birds. I couldn't believe my eyes!

Kuma looked surprised at all of the activity. He started in on the game, and I had to tell him "*No!*" several times, but was a little more hesitant about telling the neighbor kids to stop it. My heart flooded with relief when the kids finally put my feathered friends down and went home. The next day, while the kids were over, we noticed that Kuma was following the rooster around the yard. We were in the house having a snack, and I didn't think much about it. I had done so much training, and he had never bothered them before. He knew better, right? After the kids finished their snack, we went outside and noticed a few black-and-white feathers on the ground. That discovery prompted me to go looking for the leader of my flock. The kids went one way, I went the other. Shon realized what was going on and started hunting as well. I found the rooster in the front yard in his death throes. He was on the ground on his side, twitching. I called for Shon, and everyone came running.

Shon was furious. We had fed that thing for months and were counting on him to protect our seven remaining hens. Kuma was right there, head down, tail between his legs. He knew he had done wrong. Shon grabbed up that dead rooster and started beating Kuma with it. He wanted Kuma to understand that he couldn't kill our chickens. If I hadn't been so traumatized, the scene would have been rather comical. Here was Shon, my nice, calm husband, running around the yard chasing our sheepish 100-pound German Shepherd. He was swinging a huge black and white rooster by the legs, trying to make contact with Kuma, while our two new neighbor kids were watching in amazement.

Lazarus, the beautiful mean rooster, Summer 2018

The older kid, Isaac, finally spoke up while Shon was taking a brief rest in his quest for revenge and rehabilitation. Isaac said, "That rooster is still alive. I can see him blinking." How that kid could notice those little eyes blinking in all that chaos is beyond me, but sure enough! That rooster was holding onto life by a thread. Shon wasn't quite sure what to do, so he carried the battered rooster to the coop, sat the rooster up on his feet, and let him go. He staggered around a bit but stayed upright. We kept a close eye on him for a few days. He didn't walk real straight and had a hard time getting up on the perch in the coop, but he seemed to be making a decent recovery. After a week or so, he was back to his old self. I decided he deserved a name worthy of his ability to come through such an ordeal alive. I named the beautiful bird Lazarus.

Rooster Fight

I have come to realize that roosters like to protect their hens. I was in the chicken coop feeding and watering the chickens when Lazarus came at me. He got me pretty good on my leg with his talons. It was cold, so I had on jeans and another layer underneath, which helped. We were in an enclosed space, so he didn't have much room to get his momentum going before he attacked. It startled me, and I decided then and there that I had to keep my eye on that rooster. From then on, when I was feeding, I either grabbed a stick or kept an eye on him. I even used my "teacher voice" and told him that he better not try anything. My command presence worked pretty well for a while.

A few weeks after our initial confrontation, I let the chickens out to free-range. As always, I kept my eye on Lazarus, but I made a mistake. I thought he was busy pecking away at the food I had thrown on the ground, and I turned my back to him. He took his opportunity and came at me with some speed while I wasn't looking. I had a thick coat on, but he got me on my back and knocked me down. It didn't really hurt, but I was furious. It was one thing to protect his hens. It was quite another to attack when I wasn't anywhere close to his flock of girls. I grabbed the nearest stick and took off after that mean son-of-a-gun. I got several solid licks in. We seemed to come to an agreement. He wasn't going to mess with me again. We maintained this position for several months.

One lazy summer afternoon, I went to the chicken coop to check for eggs. As always, I yelled, "Hello, chickies. How are my girls?" My chickens were always so glad to see me. They got really excited. There were four eggs, so I grabbed them out of the nesting boxes and let the chickens and the rooster out to free-range. After the previous two attacks, I was well aware of that old rooster. He wasn't showing any signs of aggression, so I wasn't too concerned. There was a berm on one side of the coop that we made as a wind block. I walked around the berm and started up the hill to the house, two eggs in each hand. After I made it around the berm, I wasn't worried about Lazarus.

I don't know much about chicken psychology, but I think he was jealous that the hens were so excited to see me. He hopped on that berm when I thought I was safe. I was almost all of the way up the hill when I heard him running after me. Before I could get turned around fully, he jumped up and started his surprise attack. How can something with no arms attack like that? I can't tell you exactly what happened. It is all a big blur, but this is what I know:

1) I tripped on a root and fell down while I was trying to kick him.
2) I thought I was going to die.
3) I suck at fighting.
4) I only broke one out of the four eggs.
5) Pretty is as pretty does, and I no longer think that rooster is beautiful.

Shon heard me yelling and came running. Once again, he thought I was being attacked by a bear. When Lazarus saw Shon, he backed off down the hill like a coward. If you have ever been in a life-or-death situation, you may know that the adrenaline really starts pumping in times like these. I jumped up and told Shon about my ordeal in great detail. Shon listened patiently and then felt it necessary to debrief me after my fight. He gave me some good advice:

1) Don't turn your back on that rooster. He's mean.
2) Try not to fall down.
3) Don't worry about protecting the eggs. Just drop them and fight.

So what have I learned? I live in bear country and I can't handle a rooster.

Black Bear

One of our favorite things to do in summer is porch-sitting. With the long days, we have plenty of daylight to get all of our work done and still have time to enjoy the beauty of Alaska. The view from our second-story porch is gorgeous. On a clear day, we can see the Alaskan Range in the distance. The snow-capped mountains seem to change from day to day. On the lawn, we see robins hopping about, eating rogue strawberries that have "grown up volunteer," as my father-in-law liked to say. The swallows are entertaining in the evenings as they swoop in wide arcs, trying to snatch up mosquitoes for their supper. We join in the fight against the mosquitoes with our electric swatters, enjoying the pop the mosquitoes make when we make contact. Every summer, we have a couple of ducks who raise their little family of ducklings on Cub Lake. When we are lucky, we have a couple of trumpeter swans that make Cub Lake their home for the summer. We also see moose from time to time and especially enjoy when they get in the lake for a swim or a bath. Porch-sitting at Cub Lake is relaxing, but there is plenty to see if we look closely.

One gorgeous morning, Shon and I decided to drink our coffee out on the porch. We had our coffee in one hand and our swatters in the other. I was talking about this and that with him listening quietly when I noticed him sit up straight in his Adirondack chair. I got quiet and looked across the lake to where he was gazing intently. I knew he was right when he stated quietly, "There's a bear."

We watched as the bear ambled along the other side of the lake towards our neighbor's cabin. Roger had gone to see family in the Lower Forty-Eight, and we were watching his dog, chickens, and rabbits while he was away. He left the door of his cabin open slightly with a block screwed to the floor so his dog could go in and out, but a larger animal could not enter. As the bear drew closer to the cabin, I scanned the lake edge for Roger's dog, Lilly. The bear was still about 100 feet away from Roger's place when I noticed Lilly high-tailing it around the lake to our house. I had never seen her run that fast before. She was at our home in no time flat. I went back to looking for the bear, which had continued his trek toward Roger's cabin. Right before he got to the shop next to the house, the bear disappeared into the forest. It looked like he might have gone back behind the cabin.

After spotting the bear across the lake, Shon and I decided we better head over to Roger's cabin to check on things. Lilly was safe, but Roger also had rabbits and chickens that a bear might find tasty. I had decided that I really needed to be less complacent and more diligent after my last run-in with Lazarus. I was going through the lessons I had learned as I got ready to go face the bear. I pulled on my muck boots, grabbed my mosquito hat, and was headed out the door when I realized that I had forgotten my gun. Shon had his .45 on his hip and a shotgun loaded with slugs. I hurried back to get my weapon but decided to also get the egg basket so I could gather eggs if the bear wasn't there. No need to waste a trip. We headed to the canoe, climbed in, and pushed off, ready to go to battle … or gather eggs if the bear had passed through without stopping.

The dogs ran around the end of the lake. We kept an eye on them as they neared the cabin. Lilly, Roger's dog, was on full alert. Kuma seemed happy and wanted to play, like usual. We got out of the canoe and headed up to the front yard. We both noticed that a birdhouse was down on the ground. Shon was walking around the left side of the house with Kuma. I was still in the front yard, looking around, when Lilly came running back from the right side of the house with a horrified look on her face. Her eyes were big, and her ears were up, and she was telling me with everything she had that the bear was around the other side of the house. I started yelling to Shon that the bear was close when I saw a big, black blur run right in front of me with Kuma right on his tail.

I start yelling, "There he is!"

Shon hollered back, "Where, where, where?"

Apparently, it doesn't do much good to point and answer, "Right there," when you are out of sight of your partner.

He yelled at me again, "Where, where, where?"

When I finally remember to drop the egg basket and pull my gun, Kuma and the bear were out of sight. I screamed at Kuma to come back, but he was chasing that bear through the woods, not even an inch between his nose and that bear's butt.

I was shaking when Shon came around the corner. He told me to put my gun away as I started telling him how that bear ran right by me with Kuma on his tail and pointing the direction I had last seen them. We were worried about Kuma, but in just a few minutes, he came back to us unharmed but plenty excited. We looked around and found where the bear had been making himself at home. In the short time it took us to get over there, he had done quite a bit of damage. He had torn open one sack of dog food, overturned the rabbit feed, ripped open a portion of the chicken coop, and turned over the trash barrel. We got things tidied up, fed the animals who were all pretty traumatized, and headed home, considering what might happen next.

Protecting Property

We watched for the bear as we sat on the front porch for the rest of the day. We talked to several Alaska friends, and they all told us the exact same thing: that bear would be back. We saw how much damage he did already and didn't want him to tear up Roger's place. It was about nine that night when I gave my friend, Kay, a call while Shon and I were bear hunting in our Adirondack chairs from the porch. We chatted a while about the excitement of the day, and then Kay's husband, Robert, wanted to talk to Shon. I passed the phone to Shon as he continued to scan the area. He was listening to Robert when all of a sudden, he threw the phone in my lap and told me to talk to Robert. I didn't know why he wanted me to speak with Robert until I saw him grab the rifle.

I looked across the lake, and there he was. That bear was headed back to Roger's house for another meal. I quickly told Robert that Shon was about to shoot a bear and would call him back. Shon took a shot with his .350 Savage, and the bear went down. I was yelling, "You got him!" when that bear got up, shook his head, and started running along the side of the lake. Shon took another shot and missed him. He got one more shot off, which appeared to make contact before the bear vanished. We didn't know if he just went down in the grass or if he had made it into the forest. I called Robert back and told him we needed to go find the bear.

On the way across the lake, I was nervous about being in the front of the canoe. Being in the front meant that I would be getting to the shore first. Lilly made me feel better when she met us on Roger's dock when we got across the lake. I looked around for Kuma, but I couldn't find him anywhere. I knew he didn't like the noise from the gunshots, but he had been with us when we left the house. Shon started walking down the lakeshore toward the last place he saw the bear while I looked for Kuma. We needed that dog. I finally spotted him swimming—in the middle of the lake! For whatever reason, that silly dog decided to swim across the lake instead of running around the lake with Lilly. In all of the excitement, Kuma must have decided to stay as close to us as possible. He was exhausted when he finally got to our side of the lake. That was a long way to dog paddle. I grabbed his collar and helped haul him out of the lake. He showed his appreciation with a disgusting spray of lake water as he shook the water from his thick fur before taking off after Shon.

Lilly and I stayed next to the lake as Shon and Kuma followed the blood trail into the forest. The mosquitos were terrible. I stood there bothered by the little devils, knowing that they were the least of my worries. I heard Kuma bark a few times and could hear rustling in the underbrush. I knew the bear was in there with Shon and Kuma. I heard my heart pounding as I tried not to think about how wrong things could go with that wounded bear. Shon hollered that he found him, and then there were several shots. Kuma came out of the thick brush and stood next to Lilly and me while Shon finished killing the bear.

The older I get, the harder it is to deal with death. It was no fun seeing that bear lying dead in the forest. I tramped down the foliage in the area to make it easier for us to work. I helped by holding the bear's paws one at a time as Shon skinned the beautiful animal. It took several hours to process the bear. Being that close to a bear was surreal. I wondered about his life and what it had been like. I was sad about the necessity of killing him and was glad to know that the bear meat would be used. We were exhausted as we put the last package of bear meat into the freezer early that morning. I had to keep telling myself that he had threatened Roger's animals and property and then came back for another try. He was a danger to us all. Finally, I decided that it was better for him to be in the freezer than in my chicken coop, killing my girls.

Hunting Bears and Berries

Anytime Shon and I walked around outside during the summer, I noticed that our perspectives were utterly different. I hunted berries. He hunted bears. Living in the Alaskan wilderness helped me to see how our differences made us work better together. He had my back as I had my head down, gathering blueberries, strawberries, or cloudberries, which was one of my favorite things to do.

The blueberries and cloudberries were the hardest to harvest because they grew in the thick forest. Not only were the bears a concern, but the mosquitoes were also abundant out in the swampy woods. I wore my mosquito net hat with a bandana tied around my neck to keep the little devils at bay. A long-sleeved shirt and long pants were a necessity. The only skin that was showing when I picked berries was that on my right hand. I always wore a glove on my left hand, but it was too hard to pick the little fruits with a glove. Invariably I had lots of nasty bites on my picking hand, but it was worth it to get all of that fruit that grew wild.

Right after the bear incident, Shon went to town with a friend. It was berry season, and I didn't want to miss out on picking the delicious fruit just because I didn't have my bodyguard around. I knew I needed to be smart about my berry hunting, so I immediately squashed any ideas of picking blueberries or cloudberries out in the forest alone. Those would have to wait until Shon got back, but I might figure out a way to pick strawberries safely. I had a big patch on the runway that needed to be harvested, but I hated to be that far from the safety of the house. I finally decided to drive the Arctic Cat down by my favorite little patch with the shotgun in the passenger's seat. If a bear approached, I had the gun nearby, a pistol on my hip, and a way to get back to the house quickly. Kuma, always my fierce protector, was also there to alert me of any danger. As I sat on the ground picking, I thought about how different my life was now. I picked wild strawberries in the bush of Alaska instead of buying them when they went on sale at the local grocery store. Berries proved to be way more delicious when I picked them myself, watching for bears and fighting mosquitos, with my loyal dog nearby.

Jam

I found myself with more fruit than I knew what to do with that first summer. Ruth had ten rhubarb plants that I regularly harvested from the middle of June through August. Rhubarb looks like a red stalk of celery but tastes like a very tart strawberry. I picked, chopped, and froze the rhubarb to use throughout the year. Any food that I didn't have to haul out by plane or by snow machine needed to be utilized. I tried very hard to not let anything go to waste. I picked as many berries as I possibly could, freezing them by the quart. Kuma was even getting tired of our strawberry picking. One day he communicated his displeasure very clearly when he plopped down in the middle of my strawberry patch, demanding a belly rub. I laughed and complied, knowing that I was tiring of picking berries as well By the end of July, the strawberries were slowing down, so I was looking forward to a little break. I didn't get it, though, because the raspberries along the side of my cabin started ripening.

I never bought raspberries unless they were on sale, and even then, it was only for special occasions. Raspberries had always been a treat at my house. There was no way I was letting those precious berries fall to the ground. Kuma looked at me warily as I grabbed my berry bucket. At least I was close to the house, and he could gnaw on a moose bone while I worked. I wasn't as vulnerable because I was standing up instead of sitting on the ground. He seemed to relax a bit as I harvested the sweet fruit. I started at the north end of the house and worked my way carefully to the south. As I walked back toward the backdoor, I scanned the raspberry stalks, and it didn't even look like I had picked anything. I took my bucket in the house and transferred what I had to a bowl. As I returned for another bucketful, I decided those raspberries were ripening as I quickly as I could pick them. I never felt like I was ever finished harvesting. I could always see just a few more that I had missed.

I might not have been a useful gardener that first summer, but I more than made up for it with the wild fruit Kuma and I had faithfully harvested with Shon's help. At the end of the summer, I had a freezer full of rhubarb, blueberries, strawberries, and raspberries. (I ate all of the cloudberries, so none of them made it to the deep freeze). Shon told me that we needed to get the freezer cleaned out so we would be ready for a moose come fall. It was time for me to learn how to make and can jam. I was nervous, but like anything else, the fear faded away as Shon and I worked together to make that first batch. After a few successful jars, I mixed the fruit to create a specially blended jam that

I called Alaskan berry. I found that the rhubarb, strawberries, and raspberries worked very well together when I used my food processor to chop all of the fruit into tiny bits. There were several rainy days at the end of the summer when we canned jam, listening for each little ping that came with the successful completion of a jar of delicious jam. Before moose season, I had several dozen jars of jam lining my pantry shelves for our friends and us to enjoy during the year.

Trumpeter Swans

When the birch trees start dropping their leaves, we knew it was time for us to get everything done before winter caught us unprepared. Shon and I worked like crazy to finish our summer projects before fall, or what Alaskans call "Freeze-Up." It was hard to stay focused, though, when there were two beautiful trumpeter swans on the lake in front of our house.

I knew the swans would be heading south for winter soon, so one day in September, I decided to see how close those swans would let me get. I grabbed my camera and headed to my kayak at the lake's edge. I had to hurry so Kuma wouldn't beat me around the lake and scare them away. I paddled pretty fast until I was about halfway across the lake, and then I let my kayak just drift in their direction. The swans were well aware of my presence, getting nervous, which was evident by their honking. I started snapping pictures. They turned and started paddling down the edge of the lake, so I turned my kayak the same direction while closing in a bit. I was getting some pretty good pictures when they finally had enough. The first one took off with the second one close behind. They looked like they were walking on water for a while before they took flight. Their wingspan was huge! I could hear their wings flapping in the air as they took off. I took pictures as they made a large arc towards our house then came back towards me. They flew off through the outlet to the back lake. I was contemplating the experience and wondering about the shots I got as I headed back to the house.

Trumpeter Swans on Cub Lake, Summer 2018

Shon was watching from the front porch as I slid the kayak back to shore. I was nervous about my camera near the water but knew I hadn't ever had any trouble getting out of the kayak before. I had one foot on the land and one foot in the kayak when the kayak shifted. It had been a long time since I tried to do the splits. I started yelling for Shon to come help. He ran out of the house and started down the lawn. He was about halfway to me when my foot on land decided to slip into the lake. It was pretty deep right there, so the water went up to my right hip but I still had my left foot in the kayak and was holding the camera up out of the frigid water. Shon saw my predicament and came running. It usually is Shon who falls down, and I laugh at him, so he took this opportunity to point out that our roles were reversed. About the time Shon made his point, my sweet husband stepped in a hole and went tumbling. He did a somersault or two and it was my turn to laugh. When he finally got to me to pull me out, we were both laughing at each other.

Underwear Hunt

As our second summer was drawing to a close and the days were getting shorter, moose season was upon us. We were really hoping to fill our freezer with a moose. We had heard that moose meat was very similar to beef in taste and texture and were excited to give it a try. Shon looked every day, hoping one would come near the house. We didn't have a way to travel very far, so a moose needed to come to us. We prayed every day for God to send one our way.

Close to the end of the season, Shon decided he would try calling one in. He got a piece of birch bark, put Kuma in the house, and set out walking north of our house. Off of the end of our runway is a beautiful open area of muskeg with a beaver dam on one end. He walked three-quarters of a mile out into the opening and started his call. He used the birch bark to amplify the sound of another bull moose wanting to fight. As he walked home, he started hoping that a big bull moose didn't appear. Shon was out in the open with no cover and only his pistol on his hip. If an angry bull showed up to fight as he was walking home, he might be in trouble. As he got closer to the house and didn't see a big moose, he was somewhat relieved and resigned himself to the fact that we might not get a bull this season.

Getting a moose into our freezer would help out tremendously with our food budget, much less the hassle of having meat hauled out. And the pressure of getting a moose was weighing heavily on Shon. When I got out of bed first the next morning, moose hunting was on my mind. I knew Shon had been calling the day before, so I peeked out the window to see if his calling brought us a moose. My heart stopped when I saw a huge moose out in the yard! I started to the bedroom to wake Shon up, then changed my mind. I rushed back to the window to make sure it was a bull. Sure enough, he had a huge rack. I also noticed a cow and a calf in some brush almost out of sight. The bull was thrashing his horns in the grass and willows. It looked to me like he was either wanting to fight or was trying to impress the cow. Now that I was sure of what I was seeing, I ran to the bedroom to wake Shon. I shook him gently and said, "Shon, there is a huge moose in the front yard." He shot up out of bed like a rocket, threw on a shirt, and grabbed his rifle.

The moose was still thrashing about when Shon went out on the front porch. I watched from the window as Shon, looking rather ridiculous with no pants, steadied his rifle and took aim. As soon as Shon took that shot, the moose froze. The moose wasn't far from us, so I could see his expression when he took that first round. He looked like he knew that he had made a mistake looking for a fight at this house and my heart broke for him. Shon took another shot as the moose turned to try to make his escape. We couldn't have the moose running off into the forest or we might not be able to harvest the meat. He went down after the second shot. I found myself conflicted. I knew we needed the meat, but I had never before been so aware of the taking of a life for sustenance. I knew I wasn't going to waste any of the meat from this moose.

Shon and I had processed many white-tailed deer over the years in Texas. It only took a few hours, so I was not prepared for the amount of time and work that it took to process this moose. After Shon finished getting dressed, we headed out the door for the work that had to be done. It took us about five hours just to get the four

121

quarters hung on the front porch, and that was with Roger's help. We worked hard for the next three days putting the meat away.

Shon with his first moose, Fall, 2017

After a while, we had our process down. Shon cut big pieces of the meat from the hanging quarters and brought them to me to clean. I cleaned off the dirt and hair in the sink. Shon cut the huge backstrap into steaks. The hindquarters were cut into chunks and then canned using our pressure cooker. The front quarters we processed through a meat grinder into hamburger. The steaks and hamburger were put into freezer bags and sealed with a vacuum sealer.

We had never canned moose before and were a little nervous about trying it. I looked up the process online and we were careful to follow the instructions according to the USDA. Canned moose meat didn't look very appealing, but it was delicious. The meat cooked as it was being pressure canned and it tasted very similar to a tender pot roast. I found that having canned moose meat was a great time-saver for me. I could boil up some potatoes, onions, and carrots, add a can of stewed tomatoes and a jar of moose meat, and have a quick stew in less than thirty minutes. Shon's favorite was my Mexi-moose recipe. I combined a can of moose meat with a can of tomatoes and peppers and let it simmer on the woodstove until heated through. I added a can of refried beans and served with homemade tortillas. Canned moose has turned out to be one of our favorite meals.

We love to see the moose around our place. They are magnificent creatures that make life better for the people who live out here. They are constantly monitored by the locals. People discuss the ratio of bears to moose, since bears are predators and like to prey on moose calves. After my story got out, our neighbors have also discussed the danger posed by the man on the porch with no pants. And anytime I see Shon in just his underwear, I have to ask, "Are you going moose hunting?"

Trust in the Lord with all your heart and lean not on your own understanding; in all your ways submit to him, and he will make your paths straight.

Proverbs 3:5,6 NIV

CHAPTER 6

Snowy River

Overcoming My Fear

Fear is one of those things that we all have to face. I have learned that I fear anything I haven't done before, even if it is a simple thing like baking an apple pie. I must face my fears out in the bush because I have found myself in many unfamiliar situations. Shon has proved to be much braver than I am. I guess I shouldn't be surprised by that, since he was in law enforcement all of those years, but I never got to see him in action until we moved to Alaska. When I learned how to fly in 2006, I kept a Scripture in my pocket to help me deal with the terror that would creep into my mind and around my heart if I let it. The Scripture was 2 Timothy 1:7 KJV. It says, "For God hath not given us the spirit of fear; but of power, and love, and of a sound mind." Recognizing that fear doesn't come from God helped me to see that I must face each fear that comes my way.

I was happy to ride along when Shon first got his snow machine. When we realized that we would be much safer with a second one,

I knew that I had to face another fear. I didn't mind riding the snow machine or going through the forest on the windy trail. It was the steep incline in the Twenty-Mile Slough that made my heart skip a beat. Shon explained that I needed to be careful of my speed. If I went too fast, I would go airborne at the top of the hill. If I went too slowly, I wouldn't make it up and would find myself going back down the wrong direction. Neither one of those scenarios sounded good to me. We had traveled up the incline on numerous occasions, and I was familiar with the appropriate speed. Shon went first. He stopped his machine and turned around to watch as I made my way up.

I took a deep breath, said a quick prayer, and headed up the hill. About halfway up, I was afraid I wasn't going fast enough, so I gave it a bit more gas. I was concentrating so much on my speed that I went up the hill at a slight angle. When I reached the top, I did jump into the air a little, and my machine tipped over to the right slightly. My right foot shot out to catch myself, but it never even touched the ground. The wide skis kept me upright, and I made the turn to follow Shon. I immediately knew that I needed to be more careful when lining up to make it up the incline. It wasn't perfect, but I did it! After a few more trips, it was no problem. After a few more successful climbs up the hill, I gunned it a bit at the top and enjoyed the jump.

Where Did You Go?

Riding the snow machine was scary at first, but before long, Shon and I were both getting the hang of it. Our machines were made differently and had different functions. His was more like a pickup truck that could haul a heavy load and make it through rough terrain. I named his "The Beast." Mine was more like a sports car. My machine had a harder time going through deep snow, but if I followed Shon's track, I had no trouble. On our established trails through the forest, my machine was much faster. I got to where I loved zipping through the trails.

We took off to Skwentna for a mail run one beautiful, cold morning that first winter. I was leading, with Shon bringing up the rear. I watched as the sun rose over the gorgeous, snow-covered trees and lakes. The light was stunning that morning, with a mixture of pink, orange, and yellow. As I turned northward out of one of the seismic trails, Denali came into view. The massive size always amazed me, and it was over seventy miles away. It was breathtaking. Not only was I enjoying the scenery, but I also enjoyed taking the sharp turns as fast as I could go. It was exhilarating to travel over the bridge at Cripple Creek without even a second thought. I was enjoying my ride so much that I forgot to watch out for Shon in my mirrors.

I got to the slough and realized that my husband wasn't behind me. I wasn't sure what to do. If I turned around to check on him, we would possibly meet on our trail, which was only wide enough for one snow machine. If we were out in the muskeg, it wouldn't be a big deal because we would have plenty of room to turn around. If we met in the seismic line in the forest, there wasn't much room, and we would have a traffic jam. One of us would have to back up until we found a place where we could turn around safely. I sat there, considering all of my options. I finally turned off my machine and took off my helmet so that I could listen for the sound of his snow machine. I sat there for ten minutes or more, wondering what could have happened. He might have lost the tub along the trail and had to retrieve it. He could have gotten stuck. I was running through all of the options when I heard his engine in the distance. Relieved, I sat there at the top of the hill until he came into sight, thinking I was smart not to go back to check on him.

When Shon rode up next to my machine, he was not happy. He informed me that I had taken off like a bat out of hell, and he had trouble keeping up with me. Because he had the tub behind him, he was continually looking back to make sure he didn't lose it. Trying to keep up with me and looking back had been a bad combination. He had hit a small spruce tree on a curve. His windshield and a front panel both had ugly cracks. He wasn't seriously injured, but he was none too happy with me. There I was, feeling all smart about waiting patiently. He wasn't thinking about me being smart at all. Instead, he said, "Just because your machine goes fast doesn't mean you have to drive it like a scalded ape!" To make things even worse, he asked me if I had been watching for moose in the trail. I hadn't considered running into a moose. We decided then and there that he would lead and watch for moose. I would follow and make sure we didn't lose the tub.

Moose on the Trail

Running into a moose was a real possibility. Not too long after Shon's run-in with the spruce tree, we were on a seismic line when Shon stopped in the middle of the trail. I pulled to a stop behind him and noticed a bull moose blocking our way. Moose use our trails as much as we do. The packed snow on our path makes walking a lot easier for the long-legged creatures when the snow gets several feet deep. Our neighbors had told us to be patient with moose. They usually aren't aggressive unless they feel threatened.

We sat there, looking at the moose, and the moose looking at us. We finally turned our snow machines off because Mr. Moose didn't seem to be in any hurry. He stood there for a good twenty minutes. We laughed about our traffic jam and how much more fun this was than the traffic problems on the interstate in El Paso. We were glad that we weren't in a hurry and could enjoy the moment. The moose finally decided that he'd had enough and ambled off into the forest, making room for us to continue on our way.

Watch Out!

Our new method of Shon leading with me following was working. He went much faster, since he didn't have to keep looking over his shoulder. I still enjoyed the beautiful scenery and didn't have to worry about leaving Shon in my snow dust. He was right there, keeping me at a reasonable speed like a good state trooper.

We headed over to play racquetball across the river one morning. We made it to the slough without a problem and then made the turn onto the Yentna River. I was following along, thinking about how the temperature always dropped when we got to the slough, when Shon started pointing to his left. I slowed a bit while I looked over to see four majestic moose off in the distance. There were two bulls and two cows. When I glanced back to the trail, I saw Shon had stopped right in front of me, gazing at the moose. I slammed on my brakes. The back of my snow machine started fishtailing before it finally stopped, just a few inches behind "The Beast." He was mad that I almost hit him. I wasn't too thrilled that he stopped right in the trail.

Once more, we had to make a couple of new rules about traveling by snow machine. It took us a while to figure out that Shon never used his brakes. His machine was so heavy that he just let off of the throttle, and it quickly glided to a stop. I could usually see when he was stopping, but when my attention was on something else, the brake lights might have helped give me a heads up. We also decided that when we were on the river where the trail was plenty wide, and we were traveling at faster speeds, I would never drive directly behind Shon. And he agreed to never stop in the middle of the trail unless it was necessary. The moose didn't enjoy our rather boisterous discussion. When we looked back over, they were long gone, probably discussing issues of their own.

This new life together helped our communication skills, even if our discussions were sometimes on the lively side.

Getting Supplies by Snow Machine

Getting supplies delivered out in the bush of Alaska by snow machine was a real treat. I made lists all during the year, just waiting for the river to freeze up so I could restock my shelves. When Ken Lee said the trail was safe and he could start freighting, I made a big order at a wholesale club in Anchorage through an app and then let Ken know when it was ready for pickup. Either he or his wife picked up my order and reboxed it so it would survive the snow machine trip from Deshka Landing.

Ken worked in Eagle River during the week but delivered supplies and fuel to people along the Yentna River every weekend. One of his biggest customers was the Skwentna Roadhouse. He hauled fuel so they could sell it to snow-machine customers. The Roadhouse was the first official stop for the Iron Dog, a 2,000-mile snow machine race, and they had to have enough gas for all of the racers. On his way to Skwentna, Ken called us with his satellite phone to let us know when he was passing by the Twenty-Mile Slough. Shon and I jumped on our snow machines and headed to the river with our tub to retrieve my order.

Picking up supplies from Ken Lee, February, 2017

We only had a tub, also called a toboggan, to haul supplies, whereas Ken had several freight sleds. Our toboggan sat directly on the snow while Ken's freight sled was off of the ground by eighteen inches or so. It was made of steel with a wood deck, about three feet wide and fourteen feet long, and was on skis. The skis were articulating which made a smooth ride for anything being hauled. Ken swore that he could bring eggs on his sled and none would break. If we put eggs in our tub, we would just have a scrambled mess. I kept this in mind when making my orders. We picked up a couple of my loads from Ken before Shon made an order of his own. Shon ordered three large solar panels, and they weren't cheap.

I was nervous as we headed to the river to get our big-ticket item. I wasn't worried about Ken. It was Shon and our plastic tub that had me concerned. I had visions of shattered solar panels all along our path.

When we got to the slough, I noticed that there was some overflow. Overflow is slush that sometimes forms under the snow in warmer weather. When Shon drove through it, I saw the slushy brown mess and did my best to avoid it. We had learned that a snow machine can get stuck in overflow and can be a booger to get out. When going through it, I was aggressive on the throttle, getting through it as quickly as possible. When we got to the river to wait for Ken, we talked about the overflow and decided it wasn't deep enough to worry about.

Ken arrived, and we transferred the panels from his sled to our tub. They were in thick, cardboard boxes. Shon tightened them down on the toboggan with straps. I was nervous about the panels hitting trees along our trail, but the men assured me that it would all be okay. Shon's typical response when I am worried about anything is always, "Awww, it'll be alright." After another fun visit with Ken, we headed down the slough towards our trail.

Shon was in the lead with me following along, watching the load. When we got close to the hill in the slough, Shon hit the overflow, now with the weighty panels. I was glad I was way back when he hit it because he poured on the gas, trying to make it through without getting stuck. Overflow shot up in the air from his track, making a rooster tail that was spraying slush in a vast arc behind Shon's machine. His machine was screaming, but it continued forward through the overflow, moving very slowly. I was relieved when the front of "The Beast" made it to some good snow, and he pulled out of the slush. He made the turn up the steep hill with the solar panels following along, wet, but not stuck. Through the windy trails we went, all the way to the house. When we got home, we unpacked the expensive panels from the wet cardboard, thankful to find that they were in perfect condition.

Twelve Trips

It wasn't long before we bought a freight sled. We also purchased an old truck, or beater with a heater, to keep at the landing. Shon had watched as Ken hauled double sleds with about 2,500 pounds of cargo. He still wanted Ken to pull some of the more difficult loads, but thought he could handle a single with lighter weight. We desperately needed a new couch. The one in the cabin was ancient. My washing machine needed updating, as did the freezer. Shon ended up making twelve trips into town and back, hauling supplies that winter. He brought out roofing materials, animal feed, propane, lumber, gas, and diesel. I made the trip once that year, hauling only myself and my gear.

Shon freighting down the frozen Yentna River, February 2018

I'd made the trip to Skwentna, which was about a fifty-mile round trip. When we got to Skwentna, we had a chance to warm up, get something to eat, and rest a bit before making the return trip home. I wore my ski clothes and several layers of long johns. I had bunny boots to keep my feet warm. We had invested in useful snow machine gloves and gauntlets for our handlebars to keep our hands toasty. I bought a helmet that kept my head warm and had finally found the right combination of a balaclava and a neck warmer that completed my outfit. I was better equipped than that first trip over to Skwentna, when I'd gotten so cold. I thought I was getting the hang of things, so when Shon asked me if I wanted to make a trip to town with him, I was all for it. If I could make a fifty-mile round trip, I could surely make the fifty-five-mile, one-way trip—as long as we went in on one day and came back out the next.

We headed out before daylight, Shon in the lead, me following. I was so excited when we made a right on the river instead of a left. I got to see some new territory as the sun began to rise. The trail was in decent shape, and we made good time. Shon stopped from time to time to point out specific landmarks, but it all looked the same to me. Shon had mentioned Scary Tree several times when talking about his trips, so I was excited when we finally got to that landmark. The scary tree was long gone, but the name had stuck. It just looked like a fork in the river to me. Shon asked me how I was doing. I told him that my right hand was getting tired from gripping the throttle, and my legs were getting cold. He hated to hear that I was cold because the temperature always dropped when he made the turn onto the Susitna River.

I knew exactly what he was talking about as we veered left on the Big Su. The wind was blowing directly at us, and my legs got colder and colder. The farther we went, the rougher the trail became. It was unnerving driving over ice bridges with the river running just a few feet over. The water looked so cold, and I couldn't help but think about the possibility of sliding off into the frigid waters. We finally made a right turn toward Deshka Landing, and the trail became rougher still. The bumps were so bad, we slowed down considerably. It seemed like we would never get there as we went up and down over the heaves of ice. I was never so glad to see the ramp going up to Deshka. When we finally made it to the parking lot, Shon told me to get into our old truck and get warm while he took care of the machines. I was more than happy to comply.

I finally warmed up, and we headed to Wasilla with our shopping list. Our first stop was at the snow machine shop. Shon needed a fifty-cent part. While he was getting what he needed, I noticed a snow machine suit just my size on sale. Shon thought he was going in for a cheap little part, but we left with a $400 coat and a $400 pair of pants. Very rarely have I ever spent that much on one outfit. My wedding dress comes to mind, but that's about it. I didn't even think twice. I knew I needed better gear if I was going to make the trek back out to the house. And I had to make it.

The next day, I felt much better as I pulled on my new, more appropriate apparel. Shon and I loaded our freight sled down with our newly acquired cargo, and we headed toward home. Shon stopped several times to check to see if the load had shifted. On our way home that day, we saw several moose on the river. I saw eagles. We saw a guy walking down the river, pulling a sled behind him. I wondered where he was going. We saw several other people on snow machines, pulling loads to their cabins.

I was feeling pretty good about myself when we neared a steep bank. The fear was gone. I knew I could make it. I was even feeling a little cocky, knowing that I could catch a little air at the top. As I was climbing the incline, two guys on snow machines screamed by me on either side, jumping high into the air when they reached the top. It scared me to death and reminded me that I wasn't so hot after all.

It was growing dark when we got back to our familiar trail. I was exhausted, and my hand was cramping, but I wasn't cold. Shon's snow machine started overheating as we climbed up out of the river towards our cabin, so we stopped to let it cool. As we sat there in the dark, we talked. Life was harder for us in many ways, but we were enjoying life, and each other, so much more. Shon mentioned that we were more appreciative of a trip to the grocery store, a good night's rest, and a warm house. When his machine was finally cool, we made the last five miles of trail, happy to be together. And content to make it to our cabin on Cub Lake.

Gathering Wood

Not only did snow machines change our way of getting supplies, they also changed how we got our fuel for the woodstove. That first winter of wet wood was horrible. We needed good firewood that had been appropriately seasoned and didn't try to kill us before getting it to the house. Shon did his research about the best wood to burn, which was birch, and I asked Steve at the post office how he got his wood for the winter. With the information that we put together, we developed a new, much more effective method of getting our firewood.

By our second winter, we had a plan, and we were anxious to try it out. First, Shon and I located a hill with several birch trees on it. Birch trees don't like growing in the muskeg. They thrive on knolls that have better soil. We tried to find an area that had several trees that we could harvest in one area so it would cut down on our workload. We were all for the "working smarter, not harder" concept. We also looked at the trees carefully to see if they had any conks growing on them. Conks are a type of fungus that grow on trees when they have started rotting on the inside. We wanted healthy trees with no conks. And we wanted trees that were going to fall correctly. We learned our lesson on Forked Tree Lane and didn't want to have to deal with a cut tree hanging precariously in another tree! That's just no way to live.

After finding the perfect grove of trees, the second thing we had to do was pack down the snow. Shon used his snow machine to drive all around the hill to make the snow hard so we could walk easily. If we didn't pack it down, we could sink several feet, making it difficult to walk, much less deal with a tree. After packing down the snow, we let it set up overnight with the cooler temperatures. When we went out the next day, the snow was firm, and we were able to walk all over the hill without breaking through the snow.

As soon as it got light outside, Shon and I put on our work clothes and headed out. Shon got the chainsaws ready, put them on his snow machine, and hooked up our plastic tub. I got my machine warmed up, and we prepared to go. Kuma ran happily between us, always looking back to see if I was coming, then running ahead to catch up with Shon. When we got to the hill, we picked the tree that needed to come down first. We looked at the way the tree was leaning and which side had the most branches. After figuring out how the tree might naturally want to fall, Shon made his cuts while Kuma and I stood off behind other trees so we would be safe. When the tree finally fell, we both yelled, "*Timber!*"

Shon got my smaller chainsaw going, and we both got to work cutting the small branches off of the tree. After cutting all of the small stuff, I put my chainsaw to the side and started pulling the brush off so Shon could see what still needed to be cut. I piled the trash branches out of the way and threw any small limbs that were big enough to burn in the plastic tub. With that finished, Shon bucked the tree into about eighteen-inch rounds. As he cut them, I stood them up into the snow, bottoms up. We learned from Steve, the postmaster, that birch pieces are more natural to split when they are placed with the larger end up because of how the limbs grow. And it worked! We left the rounds to freeze standing up and headed back to the house to let nature help us in our process. After stacking the little bit of limbs on the woodpile, we headed for the house.

The next morning, Shon, Kuma, and I headed back out for our final step. Once again, we warmed up the snow machines and attached the plastic tub. This time, we threw in two mauls for splitting. I was almost as excited as Kuma when we went back to retrieve our firewood. Shon split the largest rounds close to the tree stump while I worked on the smaller rounds that came from the top of the tree. After just a few minutes, we stopped to take off our jackets. It might be twenty degrees outside in the snow, but it was hard work. My dad joked about how gathering firewood warms a person not just once, but several times, and I believe it. The wood split nicely. We had the big tree split in about half an hour and then loaded as much as we could haul in the tub. Kuma stole a piece of firewood and hid it in the forest like it was a moose bone, which made us laugh.

Kuma "helping" with wood, March 2018

"Good Wood" Pile, March 2018

We rode back to the house and unloaded our haul in the wood-shed. It was Shon's job to pick the wood up and hand it to me while I stacked it. I have learned that I am a very particular wood stacker, and Shon's stacking goes every which way. It drove me crazy. While stacking the wood, he gave me a hard time about how I liked it "just so." I argued that it was necessary so it wouldn't fall later when it dried, which he knew to be true. We knew we had to gather up all of the split wood that day so it wouldn't freeze to the ground, so we made several trips to the woodshed before calling it a day.

There was something satisfying about seeing our woodpile grow. Anytime we passed by our woodshed, one of us said, "Do you know what kind of wood that is?" and the other one replied, "That's *good wood!*" We have even considered putting up a sign on our woodshed that proclaims to the world that we have good wood. We will never forget that messy, wet wood that was so hard to split and such a challenge to get that first year we were here.

In Texas, we never had to consider a different method of doing a job because of the season. Our thinking had to change in Alaska. We learned that it was much more effective getting wood in the winter by snow machine than by using the side-by-side in the summer. We learned that two of us working together were more than twice as effective as one of us working twice as long. Working in our strengths, we recognized that one of our biggest jobs, getting about ten cords of wood a year, could be one of our favorite things to do together.

Iron Dog

Ask anyone around here who is the first on and the last off of the river and you will most likely hear one name: Ken Lee. He's a wild man. He's one of the toughest men I have ever met, even though I did tell him once that I'd fight him when he refused payment for freighting. He just gave me a look and I decided not to push it, even though I know Ken wouldn't hurt me for anything. When I think of Ken, I smile. He is loud and crazy. He makes jokes that any ten-year-old boy would love, but would make my mother blush. He is knowledgeable in all things Alaskan, especially snow machines, and is more than willing to share information. He's attempted to teach me to call a moose. He has two calls, actually. One is a bull moose wanting to fight and the other is a cow in heat. (He has a special name for the cow in heat one, but I'm not repeating it.) They are both hysterical and I can't do either without giggling. He's wrestled coyotes off of his snow machine like a bulldogger wrestling a steer off of a horse. And I know he's tapped at least one cranky bear on the shoulder. I'm always telling him to be careful, but I know it goes in one ear and out the other.

It takes someone tough and a whole lot crazy to run the Iron Dog, so naturally, Ken has done it fifteen times, winning it once with his partner, Tracy Brassard. The Iron Dog is a 2,000-mile snow machine race through the Alaskan wilderness. Each team is made up of two riders and two snow machines. Both riders and machines have to cross the finish line, even if one is dragging the other. The racers travel over 100 mph in places, which is crazy fast on a snow machine. Over half of the teams don't make it to the end. It is a brutal race, and the route just happened to be a few miles from our cabin. The last couple of years it started at Big Lake and the first fuel stop was Skwentna. Without a doubt, we wanted to witness this famous race, so we headed over on our snow machines to watch the festivities.

For native Alaskans, the scene probably seemed relatively normal. For a couple of Texans who had never experienced anything like this, it was something else. There were lots of small airplanes circling above us, mostly chase planes for the Iron Doggers. They carry snow machine parts for the racers, scout out the trail, and give trail conditions to their team there for safety missions, if needed. Other small planes brought out "looky loos" from town. They were dropped off at the small airport and BJ, a local most likely working off his beer tab, picked them up and hauled them over to the roadhouse on a freight sled. I was impressed with the sled. It had multiple benches screwed down so six to eight people could travel in relative comfort the short distance from the airport. BJ was making trip after trip, dropping off the people from town. They were easy to spot in their fancy clothes and boots. The rest of us were in our normal snow machine gear and bunny boots.

Shon and I found a place where we could see the snow machiners come in. I also kept an eye on the people from town. They were almost as entertaining as the racers. Every once in a while, we would hear one of our friends in the forest call out that a rider was approaching. Ken, who was managing the fuel stop, got the riders to slow down and directed them to the appropriate fueling station. We saw a snow machine that had already wrecked and had to be taken out of the race briefly while replacement parts were brought in from the airport. That rider and his partner were impatient to get back on the trail while the repairs were being made. Another rider came in alone and asked for a can of fuel. His partner had somehow run out of gas just a few miles from the fuel stop. A man helping with the fuel ran to a shed, came out with a red gas can, and handed it over quickly. We enjoyed watching several more racers come through over the next half hour or so when we noticed the lone racer back again, still alone, and he was *mad*. He threw the gas can at one of the volunteers and yelled, "That was diesel, you idiot!" I'm not sure how he and his partner fared in the race, but it wasn't starting out very well for them.

I'm pretty sure Ken will take at least one more shot at the Iron Dog. He and his son, Kenney, would make a heck of a team. And if he doesn't, he has two grandsons who have been racing since they were two or three years old. I don't think the Iron Dog has seen the last of the crazy Ken Lee Clan.

Iditarod

Some like it fast, others like a little slower pace. When we are traveling along the river, Iron Doggers who are practicing for the race blow by us, traveling twice our speed, motors screaming. It is a totally different story with the dog teams. They are quiet and slow, but they, too, are racers. We give them plenty of room on the trail when we see them coming. Lots of times, we stop our snow machines as they run by, practicing for the 1,000-mile race.

The Iditarod typically starts in Willow at Deshka Landing. The dog teams make their first checkpoint at Yentna Station. They then travel to Skwentna, where they bed down for their first night on the trail. Our cabin is located just a few miles from the trail as the dogs traveled up the frozen Yentna River on their quest for victory. I was so excited when I found out that the iconic race was so close to us and couldn't wait to see the dog teams go by.

I could barely contain my excitement on race day. We had been invited by our river friends to join them on the Yentna River. We knew that none of the teams were going to make it to our neck of the woods until after dark, so we ate supper before heading to the river. Rarely do we snow machine in the dark, so going through the trail after the sun went down made everything have an eerie feel to it. The lights from our headlights bounced off of trees and snow as we traveled down our familiar trail. When we reached the slough, we nosed our snow machines over the steep incline and made the turn toward the festivities. As soon as we broke out of the slough, we saw several bonfires along the river.

Lots of people from town come out to cabins and lodges along the route to watch the iconic race. It is a tradition for people to build huge bonfires along the route where people enjoy themselves while waiting for the next team. We found our friends, pulled up a stump near the fire, and had fun visiting while waiting for the dogs. We watched for the lone headlight rounding the bend, signifying a team was approaching. The laughing and talking quieted down as the team approached.

As the dogs came into view of the fire, they looked so happy. I wondered how anyone could get fourteen to sixteen dogs to be still enough to tie them together. And they all had little booties on their feet. How the heck did they get all of those booties on that many paws? Someone asked which team they were and the musher called out his name. We all cheered for the dogs and offered encouragement. One team took a wrong trail and ended up close to the bonfire. Those dogs looked so confused for a bit and I wondered how the musher was going to get out of that mess. It was amazing to see him communicate with his team. In just a little while, he had them all going the right direction and they all looked happy again. Another person told them how far they were from Skwentna, their second checkpoint. They had made it the first fifty miles of their 1,000 mile trek. Only 950 more miles to go.

Dog team racing in the Iditarod, March, 2020

For God hath not given us the spirit of fear; but of power, and of love, and of a sound mind.

2 Timothy 1:7 KJV

CHAPTER 7

Alaska Aviation and Flying Friends

Walt

Anytime we needed in or out of Cub Lake, we called Walt. He had been a bush pilot for many years and provided air taxi services to many families and lodges up and down the Yentna River. He was reliable, a great pilot, and always good for a laugh. He was as strong as an ox and could pack a plane like I'd never seen before. When I had unusually large loads, he offered to open up the sack of beans (or whatever) and pour into all of the nooks and crannies so we could haul more. I always declined. I wasn't that desperate. There was one time that I loaded down a Suburban in town. When I got to his hangar and unloaded, I just knew it was going to take two trips to get everything out to the house. I shouldn't have worried. Walt got busy and somehow managed to fit it all in his Maule, and there was even still room for me.

One day, he came out to get me in the winter. The lake had a thick layer of ice, but we hadn't gotten any snow yet. Shon and I had been all over the lake with the chainsaw, slicing down to test the thickness of the ice to make sure it was safe for Walt to land. We had a good seven inches with some places even thicker. We had two questionable spots we called "spider holes" on the west end of the lake, so we put out two cones on them to make sure he didn't drive over them with the plane. They were probably fine, but they looked dangerous. He flew out in his Maule on wheels and landed with no problem. He hadn't changed to skis yet because no one had any snow. I climbed in, and we headed to town.

I got my shopping done in Wasilla, Walt loaded the plane down with my precious cargo, and we headed back out later that evening. As we neared Cub Lake, he lined up on our runway, dropping down right in the inlet as close to the tree line as he could. When we were directly over the frozen lake, the wheels gently touched down, but they didn't want to stop. Our lake is only about 1,300 feet long and seemed to be getting shorter and shorter as we skidded along. My weight and the weight of my load made the plane act completely different than it had when Walt came to pick me up. I was trying not to panic as we slid along the ice. As we neared the cones, I realized that Walt thought it wasn't safe to pass through the cones because he started yelling, "*Oh, no! Oh, no!*"

I knew the cones were there just so we wouldn't go over the weak spots, but I was getting nervous about the quickly approaching shoreline. I started yelling, "*It's okay! It's okay!*"

We slowed down just enough for Walt to make a 180 degree turn back toward our marked runway and away from the cones and shore. By the time he had the plane shut down, it was like nothing

146

had even happened. I was shaking a bit as I exited the plane, but I quickly realized that was nothing to Walt. Pilots have a saying: "A successful landing is one where everyone walks away and the airplane is still usable." The longer I live in the bush, the more I appreciate an experienced pilot and every "successful" landing.

Don

Everyone knows Don as the kindest and oldest pilot around. He has a PA-12 and a 206 that he uses for air taxis. When we had an unusually large load, we called Don instead of Walt because he could haul more in his 206. His charter was more expensive, but it was always fun to have a visit from Don. He never had an unkind word to say about anyone and was upbeat no matter what. He's been a bush pilot longer than I have been alive, but even at eighty-eight years old, he was as sharp as a tack.

Don came to get me in his bright yellow PA-12, a two-seat airplane, one winter when Walt's plane was down for repairs. I had never flown with Don before, and his age scared me a bit. He landed on the lake early one morning, right at daylight. I climbed in and off we went. As soon as we were above the tree line heading east, I noticed some fog ahead. Don never said a word to me but was continually asking other pilots over the radio about the weather ahead. He seemed nervous, and I strained to see out of the front of the airplane towards our landing spot. When we got close to Willow, we saw that there was a wall of fog just the other side of the airport. Don made a beautiful landing, and I was thankful to be on the ground.

I spent the night in town with a friend and got two days of shopping done. The next day, I drove to Deshka Landing, where Don came to get me in his pickup truck. As always, I was nervous about the size of my load. It was a trick to fill the plane without going over. Don assured me that his PA-12 could handle it. After arriving at his house, we loaded up the plane and pulled her out of the hangar.

In just a few moments, we were in the air, directly over Deshka Landing. Don pointed out different landmarks on the ground. Instead of flying at about a thousand feet, like Walt normally did, we stayed low and followed the path of the river. It wasn't long before Don noticed some moose and turned the plane so I could see them as well. I noticed another group, and we swooped around to get a better look. As we were looking at a moose and a calf in a clearing, I saw something unusual and asked Don what he thought it was. He made a steep bank and got even closer to the ground so we could take a better look. It was a wolf, and it was stalking the cow and calf. The wolf looked up at us, and the two moose took off running into the forest. I hoped we had given that calf a fighting chance. We watched the wolf for a bit and then continued our path along the river. We saw numerous moose and had the best time on the trip back to the house.

When we landed, Shon came out with the snow machine and the tub to retrieve the load. As we were unpacking the plane, Don asked Shon if he was a helicopter instructor. Don wanted to learn to fly helicopters. I did not doubt that Don could do it, and I'd be happy to fly with Don any day, even if he's closing in on ninety.

Fishing Joe

Shon and I were working outside one beautiful winter day when a little red, four-place Pacer flew overhead. We got a lot of fly-over traffic, so I didn't think much of it until he started turning circles over our place. We hardly ever had any visitors, so I was excited when it looked like he might land. I jumped on my snow machine, with

Kuma right with me, and headed to the lake. The red airplane went out of sight, and I thought he might be landing on the bigger lake behind our neighbor. I was headed around to Dog Leg Lake when he came back into view and gently landed on our frozen runway. I was glad he shut down the plane quickly because Kuma was running toward the plane to check out our visitor.

A jolly fellow climbed out of the plane with a huge smile. Kuma seemed to like the guy okay, so I knew he was alright. I'd barely said "hello" before the guy started talking a mile a minute. It was apparent that he was familiar with our place when he mentioned Cub Lake and Bob and Ruth. When Shon drove up on his snow machine, I didn't even know the guy's name, even though he'd been talking for a good five minutes. I hadn't been able to introduce myself. I figured out shortly that Shon and I didn't need an introduction. This stranger we had never met or heard of before told us precisely who we were and that we were from Texas. He knew Shon was a retired state trooper, and that I had been a math teacher in my past life. He even knew that we had a hard time moving to the bush and had heard that we had all of our belongings at Mike and Patti's place for the longest time. The man laughed at our trouble good-naturedly. When he finally took a breath, I asked him his name. "I'm Fishing Joe!" he answered happily.

Fishing Joe came to visit us another time during the next summer. He'd bought a new airplane, a Rans, and wanted to show it to Shon. I hadn't seen anyone in a couple of months, so when I noticed the little plane circling, then lining up on our 550-foot runway, I hollered for Shon. He and I walked quickly over to where the Rans had bounced to a stop. Fishing Joe was already talking as he was climbing out of the plane, telling Shon all about his new ride. We walked to the house, I got us all something to drink, and we went out onto the front porch for a visit. I sat there, quietly, while Fishing Joe continued talking about the Rans, telling Shon what kind of plane he thought we needed out at Cub Lake. Shon asked questions from time to time. I waited patiently, trying to find a break in the conversation so I could ask about Fishing Joe's wife and granddaughter. All of a sudden, Fishing Joe jumped up and said he had to go. We walked him back to the plane as he and Shon continued to talk aviation.

When he took off and flew away, I started bawling. Shon looked at me like I'd lost my mind. "What are you crying about?" he asked.

"I was looking forward to talking, and I never got in a word."

Tom and the Bird Dog

I got a call from Tom, my racquetball partner, one summer day. He said he had a surprise for me and wanted to fly over and drop it in Cub Lake. But he had one condition: I had to write a story online, stating that I'd fished whatever it was out of the lake. Since it would technically be true and I was curious about a surprise, I readily agreed. I knew he was up to something.

Tom flew an old two-place Bird Dog with a big 230-horsepower engine. When we were over at his place, he mentioned that it was red and white in color. I shook my head and told him it was black. He grinned at me and explained. He'd had the Bird Dog for many years. Whenever he had a mishap and had to replace a piece, it came from military parts that were olive drab. He would paint the part black before installing onto the Bird Dog. After a while, his beautiful red and white plane was mostly black, so he went ahead and painted the entire thing black. It made me wonder about all of the stories that the aircraft had to tell.

Shon and I had our life jackets on and had the canoe out in the middle of the lake, watching for the Bird Dog. I could hear him before I could see him. It didn't take Tom long to make the three-mile trip from across the river. He circled a time or two, getting lower and lower. On his last pass, a big, white trash bag flew out of the plane, landing close to us. We hurried over and fished it out of the lake as Tom zoomed away, back over the river. We opened the package to find a big, beautiful, silver salmon.

Tom flying over Cub Lake in his Bird Dog, Summer of 2017

Ann holding out the salmon she fished out of Cub Lake,
Summer of 2017

Shon took my picture holding the salmon out by the lake. True to my word, I posted a picture of the salmon online with the caption, "Look what I fished out of Cub Lake." All of my Texas friends responded with "Good job!" or "Nice fish!" None of my Alaska friends said a word. They all knew that salmon didn't come out of our lake.

I realized that Tom was trying to get a reaction out of Bob and Ruth, the former owners of our home. After about three days, I got a message from Ruth, asking how in the world that salmon came out of Cub Lake. She didn't think I would lie, but they couldn't figure it out. When I explained that Tom had dropped it out of the Bird Dog and I had fished it out, she was fit to be tied. She and Bob had been wondering about that fish for three days. It all made sense when they heard Tom was involved. And I've had to explain to all of my new Alaskan friends that I'm not a liar. I really did pull that salmon out of the lake.

Wing Ding

The day started like most others that time of year. Shon and I drank our coffee, had an excellent breakfast, and then went out for our walk. It was our third fall, and we were waiting for the lake to freeze. When it froze to about seven inches thick, we would be able to have access to town again. Until then, we were just in a holding pattern. It was taking longer than we thought. It was already November 8, and the lake was completely open. I had written on Facebook that I was running low on half-n-half for my coffee, vying for some sympathy. Some of my friends picked fun at me, others felt my pain, but one friend offered to bring some cream to me.

We met Jack about a year ago when he rode over on a snow machine with Ken Lee to deliver some fuel. He had a cabin near

Ken on the river and was Ken's back-up on his delivery run that day. Jack and Shon had plenty to discuss. Jack was a pilot and owned a PA-12. After a few minutes, they realized that they had more than flying in common. They were both retired cops. They enjoyed visiting until Ken said it was time to go. Jack vowed to visit us in his plane, now that he knew where we lived. True to his word, Jack came back that winter for another more extended visit. From time to time, he would buzz us. We could tell it was him because Reba, his plane, was a gorgeous red-and-white PA-12. He also had a distinctive belly pod for extra cargo underneath that made him easy to spot.

That autumn day, Shon and I finished our two-mile walk and were getting the canoe ready when we heard Jack approaching. I wore my life vest and was preparing to retrieve the coffee creamer out of the lake when Jack made a couple of passes. We talked before he took off that morning, and he had asked about our runway. He'd initially said he was going to do an airdrop but was thinking about stopping in for a visit. I told him that it was only 550 feet, and there was a drop off at the end. I explained that we weren't insured and that other pilots said that it was a "varsity runway." Shon got on the phone and described the runway to him. Because the airstrip had a bit of snow and ice on it, we didn't think he would land. After he came around for the third pass, Shon walked to the lake end of the runway. Shon and I both prayed out loud, "Lord, keep him safe!" I was about ten feet away, taking pictures when I realized that we were going to have not only creamer but a visitor, too.

It is funny how my heart can have two conflicting feelings at one time. I was excited about getting to visit with Jack, but on the other hand, I knew the runway was dangerous. It would be my fault if something happened, since I was the one on Facebook talking about my need for cream. I snapped one last picture of Jack touching down on the end of the runway and prayed out loud, "Lord, help him!" The next thing I knew, Shon was saying, "*Oh no!*" and he started running to the other end of the runway.

Something inside of me snapped, and all I could say was "*Oh no!*" I'm not sure how many times I said it, but I said it the entire length of the runway while Shon was telling me to calm down.

I could see the tail of the plane sticking up almost straight up off of the end of our short airstrip. I wasn't sure if Jack was hurt or if the plane would catch fire. When we got to the end, here came Jack up the steep hill with my coffee creamer in his hands. I started telling him that I was stupid for wanting cream in my coffee and that I was going to drink it black from here on out. He kept telling me that it wasn't my fault. After he got me calmed down a bit, he and Shon started talking about what they needed to get the plane back onto the runway. Gas was pouring out of the tanks, and we needed to get the tail down as soon as we could.

We were all three walking to the house, Jack and Shon calmly discussing what we needed to gather up: rope, garden shears, and our Arctic Cat side-by-side. All of a sudden, I couldn't take it anymore and yelled at both of them, "*How can you be so calm?*"

They looked at me, surprised, then Jack replied, "I've been in worse situations than this. At least no one was shooting at me as I was going off the hill."

Shon chimed in, "Yeah, me too. This isn't too bad." I suddenly realized that I sucked in stressful situations.

Our neighbor, Roger, came over with his Argo. It took the four of us about two and a half hours to get Reba back on the runway. We attached a come-along to the tail wheel of the plane and our

Arctic Cat, and then Jack slowly winched the aircraft up the hill. We worried about the cargo pod on the bottom getting crunched as she came over the incline, so I ran to get a little red plastic sled that we had, and I placed it under the pod. At one point, the come-along didn't have any more room to pull, so Shon and Roger both started their vehicles and pulled her the last couple of feet over the steep hill. When she came over that last hump, I gave out a victory yell and scared all of the men. Everyone stopped, and she almost went back over. I got a quick lesson on keeping my mouth shut until the very expensive airplane was completely safe. I zipped my lips, and they finished pulling Reba to safety.

We examined that airplane all over. Reba looked great. There was a ding on the right wing, but other than that, there wasn't a scratch. All of us were thanking God for His protection of Jack and the plane, amazed at His sweet mercies. We went to the house to have lunch while everyone's nerves settled, mostly mine. A couple of hours later, Jack took off towards home. I was worried, but he was as cool as a cucumber. He texted several times *en route* and again when he made it safely on the ground. The next day Jack checked his propeller. He said when he bought the prop, it had 1/16th of a variance in it. The trip over the end of the runway had fixed that. It was perfect.

My coffee sure was good the next morning. I will always think of Jack and Reba when someone asks me what I take in my coffee. This experience will add a bit more meaning to my answer: "Just a little cream … but only if it's not too much trouble."

Ray and the Husky

I was working in the house and Shon was grooming our trail to the river on his snow machine when I got a text from our neighbor during our second winter in the bush. A plane had landed on the back lake. I had my music on while I was cleaning, so I hadn't heard the engine. How exciting! I wondered who it could be. Most of the people who knew us landed on Cub Lake. Maybe it was somebody new.

I ran downstairs to put on my snow machine clothes and bunny boots before racing outside. I started my machine and tried to be patient as I let it get warm. Kuma ran around excitedly, knowing that something was up. I was worried that whoever it was would fly away before I got over there. I didn't need to worry. As Kuma and I rounded the corner, I noticed a man talking to my neighbor, Roger, and his dog, Lilly. I also saw Shon on his snow machine coming from the other direction. We got to the stranger about the same time and he looked surprised that his arrival had brought people and dogs from every direction.

We all introduced ourselves and the pilot explained that he had come out to check on a cabin located on the lake. His name was Ray. He was somewhat concerned about his plane, a beautiful Husky, because he'd had a rough landing. Dog Leg Lake is like two small lakes joined together. Ray thought it was one big lake and hit a portion of the bank fairly hard while landing. He was looking over his plane while talking to us and dealing with the two curious dogs. As we talked a few minutes, Shon noticed that Ray's landing gear was bent slightly as he was admiring the beautiful plane. Shon pointed out the minor damage, and Ray took it well. I talked Ray into coming over to the house for lunch so we could visit with him where it was warm.

During our time with Ray, we learned that he was interested in fixing up a little cabin on the back lake for a weekend getaway. He was coming back to work on the cabin soon and asked if there was anything he could bring when he returned. I wasn't shy and told him it was always good to have fresh fruits and vegetables. I also asked him to bring his wife. I needed female companionship. Ray agreed to bring his wife, Riska, out to meet me as soon as he could. Little did we know then how all of our lives would be affected by this new friendship.

And lo, I am with you always,
even unto the end of the world.

Matthew 28:20b KJV

CHAPTER 8

Freedom of Flight!

Searching for the Perfect Plane

Shon had been discussing with Fishing Joe, Tom, and Walt about us getting an airplane for quite some time, but the hunt started when Ray came out to work on the cabin on the back lake. Any time we went over to lend a helping hand, talk always turned to airplanes. Shon and Ray spent hours talking about what kind of bush plane we needed for our lake and runway. After a few weeks, Ray and Shon started talking on the phone each morning about planes for sale in the area. I quickly realized that Ray enjoyed airplane shopping, especially when he was spending someone else's money. Before long, Ray asked Shon to ride back into town with him in the Husky so they could go look at a few they had found for sale online. Shon readily agreed.

Shon and Ray flew to Lake Louise to look at a Taylorcraft, but there were signs of corrosion in the airframe, so Shon and Ray agreed

159

that wasn't the plane for us. They flew over to Talkeetna to look at a Pacer that had flowers painted all over it. I was kind of hoping that one would work out, but the fabric needed replacing and it had too much time on the engine. They drove to Anchorage, Eagle River, Chugiak, and Wasilla looking at planes at each airport, hoping they would find *The One*—but didn't have any luck.

Ray and I were both getting frustrated when Shon finally called a guy about a PA-12 on Alaska's List. I had listened to lots of these calls. I could tell this one was promising when Shon's voice took on a different tone. Shon had been concerned about getting an airplane that would have the performance to get off of our short lake. Johnny, the owner, not only said the plane had plenty of capability, he told Shon that they could test it. He asked Shon to come into town to fly with him. After talking for quite a while about the plane, the conversation turned to their backgrounds. They were both retired pilots who had worked for the state police. Johnny had worked for the state of Alaska, whereas Shon had worked for the state of Texas. They instantly had a bond.

Ray flew Shon to town to meet Johnny and check out the PA-12. Ray and Shon were both impressed. I, too, was impressed when Johnny offered to fly out to Cub Lake so I could see it as well. He took me up, and we did a "splash and dash," or touch-and-go, on a nearby lake. The 12 climbed beautifully and had no trouble getting off of Cub Lake. Johnny let me fly from the back seat, my first time to ever fly a stick rather than a yoke. It was different, but I liked it. The fabric and engine were both in good shape. Johnny had owned the airplane for over twenty years and knew everything there was to know about it. I could tell that he loved that plane and wanted to make sure it went to a good home.

Who buys a 1947 airplane made out of tubing and fabric with a 150-horsepower engine? We did. And she was gorgeous. She was navy blue and white with an Alaskan flag on her tail. The plane had many modifications to make her perform better in tight spots, including the 150-horsepower engine instead of the standard 100 hp. She also had added flaps. The landing gear and tail feathers were from a Cub. Floats, wheels, and skis came with the plane, making her flyable in all seasons. Her name was N3227M, but we called her Blue.

She changed our life.

N3227, Summer of 2018 Photo Credit: Roger Bickleman

Float Rating

During the process of buying the PA-12, Shon talked to several people about getting a float rating, including Johnny. Johnny knew a guy from his neighborhood, Mike, who was a high-time Alaskan pilot and accomplished instructor. He didn't do much instructing any more, but Johnny talked him into giving Shon some training. Johnny also offered Shon a place to stay. He had a futon in his hangar and told Shon he could sleep there while he was in town. It was all set.

Johnny flew Blue out to Cub Lake to pick Shon up one beautiful summer day in July. Shon was so excited about climbing back into the pilot's seat. My husband doesn't show much emotion, but I could tell that he was raring to go. I was staying home with Kuma to keep things going at Cub Lake. When Shon jumped onto the floats and climbed into the plane, Kuma was concerned. He didn't know what to think of that big bird. Johnny had one foot on the floats and one foot on the bank. As he was pushing off the bank, Kuma grabbed his calf in his mouth and gave it a little squeeze, just enough to let Johnny know that he wasn't happy about him taking Shon away.

Kuma and I watched the plane until it had disappeared entirely and then headed back to the house. I got updates every night that week Shon was away. I hadn't heard this much excitement in Shon's voice in a while, and it was contagious. He was having so much fun flying again. He loved float flying. It opened up a new dimension to flying that he had never experienced. He was taking off and landing on lakes. And he enjoyed the challenge of getting on and off the water in the shortest distance possible.

I enjoyed talking to him about flying. It reminded me of all those years ago when we were learning to fly together. I asked him question after question about the procedures. He told me about glassy water landings. We discussed how to tell which way the wind is blowing when there isn't a windsock to indicate wind direction. He had landed off-airport in his career as a helicopter pilot, but never in a plane on a lake. It was new, and it was exciting.

Shon was also enjoying getting to know all of the pilots in Johnny's neighborhood, which I found out later was an airplane community. The community was built around a large lake and has a private grass airstrip. Most of the people in that area have a hangar and/or an airplane sitting in the front yard. They were all friendly and wanted to get to know the crazy Texan who had moved to the bush. They all had stories to share of crashes and near misses. They had lots of advice for Shon about flying in Alaska, and I could tell that he was eating it up.

Shon and Johnny with N3227M, Summer of 2018

After he had the required instruction and was proficient, he made an appointment with the FAA Examiner for his check-ride. The examiner happened to be our good friend, Walt. One might think that Walt would take it easy on Shon, but that was not the case. In fact, Walt told Shon he better be prepared, because he knew what kind of flying Shon would be doing, coming in and out of Cub Lake. Walt questioned Shon for about three hours before they ever got into the plane. After the interrogation portion, they finally went flying. Walt had Shon land on several lakes, some with obstacles on each end. He had him set up a glassy water landing. He pulled the power and had Shon land with no engine. Walt had Shon demonstrate sailing and docking, which are typically skills for boating but are also necessary for float flying. He also had Shon land on a river with a current, which was completely different than on a lake. Walt wanted to see that Shon could do step turns and step taxis, which occur when the plane gets to going fast enough that it pulls up onto the top of the water. When they were finally finished with the check-ride, Walt told Shon, "Tell your instructor that he trained you well."

Kuma and I were thrilled when Shon came home in our "new" 1947 plane. I was excited that we had a way to get around. As much as I enjoyed our solitude, it would be great to be able to get to town when we needed something. We had lived in the solitude for two years. Now we could visit our friends across the river in the summer, not just when we could ride over on our snow machines. And it wouldn't be long before I was in that pilot's seat, too. Having an airplane finally meant we had the freedom to fly.

Fish Wheel

On our first trip in the new plane, we went over to see Tom and Pat at the Bentalit Lodge across the river. It was so good to see my racquetball partner and his sweet wife. We landed on Mud Lake. Tom was there to meet us and drove us up to the lodge on his four-wheeler. We had lived in the neighborhood for two years and had never seen that side of the river without several feet of snow. It was gorgeous.

Miss Patty took me over to show me her vast garden, and we were even invited to dinner. We ate fried halibut and fresh veggies, all Alaskan-harvested. Before we flew home, Tom put us on the calendar for the "fish wheel." I couldn't wait!

The fish wheel was available to be used in the last two weeks in July to catch salmon. Tom built his fish wheel years before and made it available for residents in the neighborhood to use. When our turn came, we flew over, landed on Mud Lake, and then got into a boat. We had no idea what we were doing, so Tom and his grandson, Liam, agreed to be our guides for the day. As we traveled across Mud Lake, down Lake Creek, and out to the Yentna River, I was amazed by how different everything looked in the summer. I had only seen these areas in the winter on my snow machine. It felt weird to be boating over what had felt like solid ground before. I regretted not bringing a bigger coat by the time we made it across the river to the fish wheel.

The fish wheel was a funny looking apparatus. It reminded me of a paddleboat. Instead of paddles, though, it had baskets that turned around and around in the river. Tom told me to get in a boat next to the wheel with Liam and handed me a big fishnet. He stood on the bank with Shon, waiting for our first salmon to appear. All of the men were quiet, so I followed suit. I had a million questions, but I tried to play it cool. The wheel and the water made a rhythmic noise that was loud enough that a person had to yell to be heard, so I stood there quietly, waiting for something to happen.

In about ten minutes, a salmon surprised me when it flew out of the basket towards me. I completely missed it with the fishnet, and it landed in the aluminum boat under my feet. Before I knew what was happening, Liam popped the salmon on the head with a fish bonker. He hollered at Tom, telling him what kind of salmon it was.

Tom made a mark in a book to keep track of what we caught then proceeded to show Shon how to clean the fish. In just a few minutes, we had the fish filleted and put into the cooler we had brought along. I asked Liam how he could tell what kind of salmon it was, and he explained the different markings of the silvers, reds, and pinks. He let me know that we were just going to keep the silvers and reds. Pinks were going to be thrown back into the river. Liam also told me that I needed to snatch the fish in the net if I could so the filets wouldn't be damaged hitting the boat. Now I knew my job: catch the fish and identify them by their markings.

After all of the excitement of the first salmon, I was on high alert for a few minutes. It was difficult keeping my focus with the rhythm of the water and the baskets lulling me to sleep. I had just about decided that there were no salmon in the Yentna River when I spotted another one in one of the baskets. This time, I caught it in the fishnet and laid it down gently in the box before Liam conked it on the head. Again, he yelled out what type it was. It looked exactly like the last one, so I had him go over the markings once again. We passed off the fish to Shon right when another one came flying at us. I was determined to understand the markings, so Liam was pointing out the identifying marks when another salmon came flying out of the fish wheel, almost hitting me in the head. I squealed, and all of the men got a good laugh at my expense. With each fish, Liam held it out so I could try to identify it. I never could. Every once in a while, I guessed correctly, but they all looked the same to me.

Since I was a failure at identifying the salmon, I asked Liam if he would like for me to take over the fish-bonking duties. He handed me the club, but he looked dubious. When the next salmon came in, I waited for him to tell me if it was a keeper or not. When he said it was, I leaned down and gave it my best shot. I couldn't hit it to save my life. That salmon was flopping around like crazy. I tried to hold it down with one hand, but it was slippery. And I had to keep my eye on the basket so another salmon wouldn't fly out and bonk *me* on the head. I hit all around it, but could never make contact. Liam finally took the club and got it on his first whop. He never offered the club to me again, and I didn't ask for it back.

After about four hours, our cooler was full of thirty keepers, which turned out to be about fifty pounds for us to enjoy throughout the year. We flew home, happy to have made such a haul. When we got back, we carefully cleaned out the plane so the smell of salmon wouldn't attract bears. Tom told us before we took off that he had heard of bears tearing a plane apart because of the lingering smell of salmon. We couldn't have that. We were enjoying our plane too much to let that happen.

The fishwheel on the Yentna River, July, 2018

Tom mending nets, July, 2018

Potato Picking

Potatoes grow really well in Alaska. Tom and Miss Patty plant several different varieties in the summer on a patch of land next to their runway near Bentalit Lodge. And I'm not talking about a few potatoes. They put out about 600 pounds of seedlings. When fall comes, there are enough potatoes to feed the entire river community for the year! During the first part of September, they invite neighbors from up and down the river to the annual potato pickin' picnic. Tom and Pat have been having the potato pickin' for the last fifteen years, so all of the neighbors know to keep their calendars free. We knew about it but hadn't been able to attend until we got the PA-12. I was looking forward to seeing the harvesting of the potatoes, but I was more excited about being around *people*.

The water level at Mud Lake was low, so Tom told us to land about a mile away on a nearby lake. He arranged for one of his neighbors who was coming that way in a side-by-side to pick us up. Our neighbor, Roger, also wanted to pick potatoes, so Shon flew me over first and then returned for his next passenger. When we all made it to the designated spot, we climbed in the six-wheeled vehicle for the bumpy trail ride to the runway. I was shocked when we turned the corner and about forty people were milling around. There were several neighbors I knew, but quite a few that I did not. There were several planes on wheels lined up at the end of the runway, and people were already digging through the dirt, looking for the potatoes.

Shon, Roger, and I put on our gloves and got started. Tom came through with a tractor to turn up the soil, so it was easier to find the potatoes. We didn't have to dig. We just picked the potatoes up off of the freshly tilled soil. Tom and Pat had twenty milk crates that they wanted to be filled with seed potatoes for the next year and several more containers to be filled for their personal use. After we all had Tom and Pat's potatoes taken care of, we filled our gunny sacks with several varieties. I had never seen so many kinds. There were white potatoes, Yukon golds, reds, and a couple of different purple potatoes.

While we were working, a small airplane flew over and lined up on the runway. The little red Piper Pacer bounced to a stop, kicking up the dust in the air. We were happy to see Fishing Joe climb out with his gunny sacks. And of course, he had plenty to say to everyone.

It was fun visiting with our old friends and meeting some new ones. I was drawn to the only kid who lives out here, Joey. He was eleven years old. We talked about the books he had read while we went up and down the rows on our knees.

Neighbors at the Potato Pickin', September, 2018

Tom on the tractor at the Potato Pickin', September, 2018

Fishing Joe talking to Roger at the Potato Pickin', September, 2018

Around noon, we all took a break for lunch. There were hamburgers, hot dogs, and all of the trimmings, but the best was the French fries. Someone brought a fryer and was busy frying up the freshly harvested potatoes as fast as they could. I got a plate and found a seat next to a friend that I hadn't seen since winter. It was terrific talking face-to-face with a woman. She lived in a cabin several miles down the river and didn't see many people, so she was ready to talk as well. We laughed about having a conversation that didn't involve a generator. (The men out here talk about generators a *lot*.)

After lunch, we finished our work and everyone had plenty of potatoes to take home with them. The neighbors carried away about 1,200 pounds. Shon, Roger, and I had about 100 pounds. Tom and Miss Patty ended up with about 800 pounds leftover to send to the food bank in town. What a haul! We were glad we had a ride when we hefted up our heavy gunny sacks into the six-wheeler for the mile ride back to Blue.

Shon and Roger flew away, leaving me alone in the wilderness to contemplate the day. I lay back in the grass with a bag of potatoes as my pillow. As I enjoyed the quiet, my thoughts turned to how the airplane had changed our lives. We were able to join in the community activities or take a trip to town for groceries when needed. We could fly for the fun of it. The airplane had given us a sense of freedom that we hadn't experienced in a couple of years. Life was changing, and it was getting better every day.

Landing on Lake Chelatna

As I cleaned house one morning late that summer, Shon came into the kitchen and started making sandwiches. "What are you doing?" I asked. Shon doesn't ever make sandwiches.

"I'm taking you on a picnic," he answered with a grin.

I didn't want to fight the mosquitoes, so I just looked at him, none too thrilled. My lack of enthusiasm didn't deter him, and he continued putting our lunch together.

"Do you remember saying you wanted to see the Kahiltna Glacier?" I nodded my head.

"Let's go take a look at it and then find a lake nearby to eat our lunch."

I finally realized that we were going in the airplane. That changed everything. This was going to be *fun*.

I threw the picnic lunch in the compartment behind my seat and climbed into the plane. In just a few moments, Shon started Blue, and we were making circles in Cub Lake, waiting for the engine oil to heat up. After Shon did the run-up, we taxied to the East end of the lake. Shon turned the plane towards the outlet, throttled up, and we were quickly off the water. I loved seeing the view change. When we broke out above the trees, the mountains came into view. Instead of seeing just a few hundred yards from the ground, I could see for miles and miles from the air. It was gorgeous.

We made a turn to the northwest and headed towards the Yentna River. At the river, we made a turn to the east, looking for the mouth of the Kahiltna River that breaks off from the Yentna. When we got to it, we turned northward, meandering over the river. We knew it would lead us to the glacier. We had never flown this direction, so it was fun finding little cabins along the way. We spotted an old school bus out in the wilderness and wondered how it had gotten out in the bush and who went to the trouble of hauling it there. As we got further north, I took pictures of the mountains. Denali was out in all of her glory. The closer we got, the more beautiful it all was. The glacier was spilling out of a canyon on the south side of Denali. It was breathtaking. I knew that the pictures I took with my camera would never do it justice, but I took picture after picture, trying to preserve the moment.

Shon noticed on the GPS that there was a massive lake over the ridge, and he suggested we head over to it for our picnic. I agreed, knowing we only had a limited amount of fuel. I kept snapping pictures as Shon made his way to the lake. When we topped over the ridge, we were shocked! It was huge. I had never in my life seen a lake that big. It was stunning, and the mountains surrounding it made it even more gorgeous. It took my breath away. Shon had found the perfect picnic spot. "Will this do?" he asked, knowing that I was enjoying every minute of it.

There was not a hint of wind, and the water was perfectly still. I knew that Shon would need to set up a glassy water landing. I quit oooh-ing and aah-ing so he could concentrate on safely getting the airplane on the lake. Shon had plenty of room, since the lake was seven miles long. He set us up with a descent of 150 feet per minute with full flaps slowing the airplane. I looked out at the land to my right and could see that we were quite a ways above the water. When I looked straight down at the water, it looked like we were about to touch down. I understood then what a glassy water landing was all about. The water, when completely still, was deceiving. Our depth perception was gone entirely. It was worse than we had ever experienced because we were so far away from any land. I held my breath until I felt the plane gently make contact with the water. Shon pulled back the power and said, "Now *that* was a glassy water landing!"

We coasted to a stop, and Shon shut down the plane. He climbed out on the floats, but I was intimidated by all of that water. It was a beautiful emerald green. It had an unusual look to it, almost milky. It was quiet on the lake, but we could hear water flowing from the mountains. Shon finally talked me out of the plane, but I held onto the wing struts for dear life. I felt silly because I walked all over the floats regularly. That milky green water made me feel like it could swallow me up. Shon laughed as I took pictures while I continued my death grip on the struts. After getting some good shots, I climbed back into the safety of the airplane. We pulled out our lunch and were eating when I had a horrifying thought: What will we do if this plane won't start? I fought back the fear and decided to just enjoy the beauty. I'm not sure how long we sat there, soaking up the majesty of our beautiful surroundings.

The Kahiltna Glacier, Fall of 2018

Chelatna Lake, Fall of 2018

Our picnic spot on Chelatna Lake, Fall of 2018

After a while, Shon asked if I was ready to go home. I could have stayed there all day, but I was anxious to see if the plane would start. I could tell Shon was getting a little antsy about it as well. There was no need to worry. Blue cranked up on the first try. Once again, we pointed the plane in the direction of Cub Lake, heading home with our hearts full.

A Trip into Town

I had an English teacher in junior high I just loved. She was a little crazy, always had a smile and something funny to say. She was an encourager. The administration moved her up to high school at the same time I promoted, so she was my teacher for a couple more years. Through that, we got to know each other pretty well. As a teenager, I found myself looking to her for guidance when I wasn't sure what to do. After I graduated from high school, we stayed in contact. She even came to see me after I had my first son, about seven years after

I'd left my hometown. Over the years, however, we lost touch. When Facebook came along, she was one of the first people I tried to find. After living in Alaska for about a year, I saw her comment on one of my friend's posts on Facebook. I was so excited to see her after so long and immediately asked to be her friend. I went to her page and saw that she had lots of posts about Alaska. I figured she had been on an Alaskan cruise.

When Kay accepted my friend request, I couldn't wait to tell her that I was living in Alaska. Little did I know that she was looking forward to telling me the same thing. She was living in Wasilla with her husband, Robert. The next time I went to town, we met for coffee. We picked up right where we left off and had the best time sharing our Alaskan adventures and reminiscing about old times. She ran around town with me while I gathered supplies. Every time I went to town, I stayed with Kay and Robert. They even made a key to their place for me. They treated me like family when I was really missing mine. And I felt like we were family because we had such a history together. Shon and Robert became fast friends, as well. Robert was an airplane mechanic/pilot and had law enforcement in his background. They had plenty to talk about when we all got together.

After we got our airplane, Blue, Shon asked me what I wanted to do for my upcoming birthday. I decided I wanted to go out to eat with Kay and Robert in town. I anxiously watched the weather. As my birthday approached, the weather turned bad. It rained all week before my special day, so I had about decided that it was going to be a no-go. On the morning of my birthday, there was a break in the weather, so Shon told me to load up. I was so excited! We skirted around the clouds but made it to Seymour Lake with no problems. I had a list of supplies that I wanted to get before dinner, so we hit

Ann with Kay, her 7ʰ grade English teacher

the ground running. We got our shopping done and met Kay and Robert for an early dinner. What a treat! Not only did we enjoy the food, but we also enjoyed the visit with good friends. When we left the restaurant, a light mist was falling so we had to hurry to the plane before the weather kept us on the ground. We loaded up quickly and made it off of Seymour Lake before the skies opened up with the rain.

Having an airplane had changed our lives so much. I wasn't nearly as concerned about having enough provisions. And it was awesome that we could eat out once in a while. It had opened up our world, and we were enjoying every minute of it.

Wounded Heroes

We had friends out in the bush, across the river, but we didn't really know many people in town. We knew Kay and Robert, and we were getting to know Ray and Riska better all of the time. Kay and Riska laughed about being my only "town friends." That all changed, though, when we bought our beautiful 1947 PA-12, Blue. We didn't know it came with a neighborhood. Johnny pulled us in and made us a part of his circle of friends in the Meadow Lakes community. Shon met most of the men during his weeklong stay during float training, but I didn't meet everyone until we went in to help with Wounded Heroes.*

Wounded Heroes is an organization out of Kentucky. Johnny and a friend of his arrange a yearly trip for police officers, firefighters, or military personnel who have been wounded to come up and enjoy Alaska for two weeks. They fish, they fly, and they ride the train, along with lots of other fun adventures. Right after they get off the plane from Kentucky, the group goes to Johnny's hangar, where the neighborhood gathers to welcome the heroes to Alaska. Because Shon was retired law enforcement and our son is in the military, he knew we would like to be involved. We flew in, looking forward to being a part of such a worthy cause.

We flew to Seymour Lake early in the day so we could help Johnny sweep out his hangar and get things prepared for the festivities. Johnny enjoyed serving typical Alaskan food. People from the neighborhood brought halibut, salmon, pike, and sourdough bread. Johnny cooked up enough moose burgers to feed everyone. There were rhubarb desserts and even homemade rhubarb wine. There was plenty of food and lots of laughter. Two of the younger visitors from Kentucky questioned Shon about our life out in the bush. I enjoyed listening as the stories turned to law enforcement. Shon and the two young men exchanged tales about chases and gun battles.

---

*For more information about Wounded Heroes, go to
www.kentuckywoundedheroes.net.

The conversation eventually turned to how the two young men had become eligible for the trip. Somehow there seemed to be healing in the telling.

Shon and I had a fantastic night. We'd each brought a small backpack of belongings and had planned on sleeping on the futon in Johnny's hangar. We were visiting with one of Johnny's neighbors, FBI Billy, who asked us where we were staying the night. We pointed to the futon over in the corner. He shook his head and insisted that we come to his house. He said he had a perfectly good guest room and would love for us to stay with him. I'd only met the guy a few minutes before and couldn't believe he would invite us into his home. Shon and I weren't sure when the hangar would finally clear out so we could go to bed, so we took Billy up on his offer. We grabbed our gear and walked with the retired FBI agent to his home about a block away.

After a good night's rest, we continued our visit with Billy over a cup of coffee the next morning. I was glad we had taken him up on the guest room. It had to have been more comfortable than the futon. And I thoroughly enjoyed Billy's calm demeanor. He reminded me quite a bit of Shon: strong, easy-going, and kind-hearted. He and Shon talked about law enforcement and flying. FBI Billy also had a cabin out in the bush, so he understood the difficulty of traveling and gathering supplies. When we were getting ready to leave that morning, Billy surprised Shon and me when he told us that he was going south for the winter, and we were welcome to stay in his home anytime. Shon and I thanked him, knowing that we would never stay at his house without him being there. Who invites complete strangers to stay in their home when they aren't even there? FBI Billy did. And I will forever be thankful. None of us knew what lay ahead and how much his offer would mean to us.

Even youths grow tired and weary, and young men stumble and fall; but those who hope in the Lord will renew their strength. They will soar on wings like eagles; they will run and not grow weary, they will walk and not be faint.

Isaiah 40:30, 31 NIV

CHAPTER 9

The Crash

Floats to Wheels

Winter came late our second year in the bush. We appreciated every warm day, knowing that winter was on its way. The mild temperatures allowed us to enjoy an extended floatplane season. Shon had been flying our 1947 PA-12 on floats since July. On Wednesday, October 24th, he left me out at the cabin at Cub Lake to take care of things while he flew to Seymour Lake. Johnny and Mike had offered to help him with the float change. Mike was also going to be Shon's instructor for his tailwheel endorsement. Shon needed that endorsement so he could fly the plane on wheels or skis.

Shon flew in that evening and spent the night on the futon in Johnny's hangar. The next morning Shon, Mike, and Johnny pulled the plane out of the water at Mike's house and got busy making the transition from floats to wheels. It was Shon's first time to make this transition, and he enjoyed learning the process. After several hours of work, the PA-12 looked like a different bird. The floats were off, and the wheels were on, the nose sticking up higher into the air with the tail resting on the small wheel at the rear.

Figuring out when to make the transition from floats to wheels is always a big guess. Shon felt pretty good about his timing when the temperatures plunged one day after pulling our plane from the water. Our aircraft was high and dry, but there were many other planes at Seymour Lake that needed to be pulled out of the freezing lake. Shon's tailwheel training was delayed several days as he helped Mike and Johnny get a few more neighborhood planes out of the water. By the last day, Johnny was using a paddle to break a layer of ice that had formed around his floats so he could get his plane up on the bank.

Tailwheel Training

On Saturday, Shon and Mike finally got started on the tailwheel training. Shon and Mike took off from Leisure Wood Airstrip, located in their neighborhood. This grass strip is seventy-five feet wide and 1,800 feet long and is used by everyone in the little airplane community. They flew over to Willow Airport and did tailwheel training for about an hour and a half. After about twelve landings, they returned to Leisure Wood Runway. Due to the wind, they landed on the downhill slope of the runway.

As soon as they touched down, Shon realized he didn't have any brakes. Mike and Shon were both standing on the brakes, but nothing helped. When they got to the end of the runway, the plane had slowed down enough to make the sharp turn onto the road at the end of the airstrip. They coasted to a stop on the street without tipping over or spinning around. Thankfully, no one was coming down the road at that moment, and there was no damage to the plane. Johnny came over with a four-wheeler and towed our aircraft to his hangar so they could work on the brakes.

The next day the weather turned bad. It snowed for a couple of days, and he didn't get to fly. He and Johnny rebuilt the brake calipers to take care of the brake issue. While they were weathered in, they decided to do some other work on the plane. There were some minor oil leaks in the engine and a couple of lights that needed some attention. A navigation light and a landing light were both on the blink, so they spent the time troubleshooting until they finally figured out what the issue was. It felt good to get all these little problems fixed, and Shon enjoyed learning more about the plane. Johnny was a great mechanic and teacher. They decided to check compressions on the cylinders while they had the time. Compressions were great. They tested the spark plugs and rerouted some wiring to address an unusual drop in the RPM's on the left magneto. Shon was frustrated at the time delay, but he was glad to have the time to go over the plane so thoroughly. He knew he had a good, reliable airplane. His confidence in our aircraft had never been greater.

Tuesday finally brought some favorable flying weather. Mike came over to Johnny's hangar. He and Shon jumped in the plane, fired it up, and taxied over to Leisure Wood Runway for Day Two of training. They took off and returned to Willow for twelve more landings. Training was going very well. Mike even commented on the performance of the steady engine. After several trips around the pattern, Mike told Shon to taxi to the hangars to let him out. It was time for him to go solo. Shon made three trips around the pattern before returning to pick up Mike. They talked for a while about some springs that had come loose on the tailwheel during the last landing. When they were reconnecting the springs, Shon noticed a rip in the fabric on the left tail feather. It took them a while to figure out that they had damaged it while leaving Johnny's hangar. They had caught it on some rebar stakes that he had set out along the edge of his driveway. They flew back to Leisure Wood, where Mike signed Shon's tailwheel endorsement. Shon and Johnny spent the next several hours patching the fabric.

What else could go wrong?

Preparing to Land at Cub Lake

I was lonely at Cub Lake. I was ready for my husband to get home. I called my family and friends. I also worked on a quilt and started a puzzle to stay busy. I took a walk every morning with my faithful Kuma. I even worked on my racquetball swing. What we thought would take three or four days was dragging out to twice that amount of time. The weather changed, and I was worried about Shon getting home. I knew our airstrip, only 550 feet long and forty feet wide, was challenging, and Shon had his tailwheel endorsement for only a day. I trusted that he wouldn't try landing here if he wasn't ready, but I was also afraid that the desire to be home might make Shon take an unnecessary risk. Hearing about the brake issues made me nervous. What if he couldn't stop and went off of the end of our runway with no help close by? I was trying not to worry but found myself praying for Shon's safety quite often. I was glad when Shon called and said that he was going to do some more practice at Ray and Riska's airstrip.

When Shon called Ray to see if he could practice at his private airstrip north of Willow, Ray readily agreed. Shon filled up with fuel before leaving Seymour Lake and flew over on Wednesday morning, which was Halloween. Shon and Ray marked off 500 feet by placing cones at both ends of the designated part of the airstrip.

Shon made landing after landing that day. He enjoyed the view as he was practicing. When Shon took off of Ray's runway, he flew off of a bluff overlooking the Susitna River. As the land was dropping off below him, he enjoyed seeing the river, which was two and a half miles wide at that point. There were large islands of land covered with cottonwood trees in the braided river below him that separated the central part of the river from the various sloughs and channels. With the sudden drop in temperatures over the last week, the river had started the process of freezing. Shon noticed large chunks of ice floating downriver, many the size of refrigerators. He knew that it would take a few more days of freezing temperatures before the river below would freeze over. With each trip around the pattern, Shon enjoyed the scenery but concentrated on the job at hand. His goal was to perfect his landings to within 500 feet. At the end of the day, he knew he still had some work to do.

After staying the night at Ray and Riska's house and enjoying one of Riska's great breakfasts, Shon got a call from one of our friends who lived out in the bush. Craig had blown a transmission line on his dozer and needed transmission oil. He asked Shon if he would mind bringing the oil out to him. Craig had recently built an airstrip on his land right off of the Yentna River at the big bend. Shon was glad to have another runway to practice on and was happy to help a neighbor, so he agreed. A friend of Craig's brought Shon the oil, and Shon headed upriver to deliver the load. Shon flew the twenty minutes to Craig's airstrip and made a bouncy, but safe, landing. He handed over the oil and had a short visit with Craig before flying back to Ray's.

After practicing several more landings, Shon decided he wasn't comfortable enough to risk landing on our airstrip. Freeze-up was just a few days away, and Shon was ready to come home. Ray offered to take him back to the cabin on Cub Lake in his Husky while our plane would remain at his house until our lake was frozen enough to land there. Shon called me to let me know that Ray was going to bring him home, and we would get the plane after Freeze-up. I was relieved but also concerned about Ray landing on our short strip. Shon assured me that it would be fine but that it might be an hour or more before he got home. He still needed to unload our plane. He had some groceries, some paint, and his clothes that needed to be transferred into the Husky as soon as Ray got it warmed up.

My hubby was coming home, but I had a bad feeling. I texted my friend, Kay, and asked her to pray for his safety. She texted back and said that she and Robert would pray.

Right after Shon got off the phone with me, Ray told Shon it would take about an hour for him to get the frost off of his wings. He suggested Shon go make a couple more trips in the pattern while he got his plane ready for the quick trip out to our house. Shon climbed back in the plane, glad to have the time for just a couple more touch-and-goes.

Thirteen Seconds

Transitioning from floats to wheels made the airplane perform better because of the decrease in drag. Planes also do better at cooler temperatures, and it was a very crisp seventeen degrees. Needless to say, Shon loved the increased performance of our sweet airplane that day, even though he was frustrated that he wasn't comfortable with the super-short landings. When he left Ray's strip for two more trips around the pattern, our plane was climbing like a homesick angel at 1,500 feet per minute. He gained about 400 feet altitude and started to throttle back to 2500 RPMs from 2700 RPMs.

As soon as he pulled back on the throttle, the engine backfired and died. Shon hoped the engine would restart because the propeller was continuing to turn because of the wind caused by the forward motion of the plane. His first thought was that he would get the engine back. Shon's training kicked in, prompting him to go through his emergency procedures. He lowered the nose to glide speed, pulled the carb heat on, and switched the fuel selector to both tanks. Nothing helped, and he realized that he was going down.

He had thirteen seconds from the time the engine quit until he was on the ground. After going through the emergency procedures, his first thought was finding a place to land. He had only two possible options. He could land in a slough off of the Susitna River or try to find a break in the cottonwood trees on the island below him. He knew that the slough was going to be a stretch, and he would have to extend his glide to make it. It also had huge chunks of ice flowing in it. The water was inviting because there were no trees to hit, but he knew he could not last long in the freezing river if the plane ended upside down. Shon decided that the only option was to try to find an opening on the land.

He saw a small clearing, but it wasn't wide enough to enter without hitting the wings. Shon kept slowing the plane down by pulling back on the stick, careful not to stall the aircraft. He just hoped that he wouldn't be hitting a tree dead on. Right before the first impact, the propeller quit turning. When the right wing hit the first tree, he heard a terrible noise, and the airplane spun around. Then the left-wing hit. The next and last thing he remembered was looking straight at the ground as he was falling.

In the next few moments, he found himself sitting in the plane, everything still, except for the spinning of the gyros. Gasoline was leaking from both tanks. He turned off the master switch, hoping the airplane would not catch fire. The left window was busted out, and the windscreen was broken. Both wings were collapsed, and the door was jammed shut. It was a critical situation, but he was still alive.

Shon found his cell phone in his left breast pocket. He called Ray to tell him that he had crashed. Ray and Riska had both heard the engine stop, had already called for help, and were headed from their house to the bluff to see if they could find him.

They couldn't see him in the trees. Ray told Shon he was going to get in the Husky to find him so he could identify his exact location when help arrived. Ray informed Shon that the Rescue Coordination Center had already been called, and a rescue team was on the way. After Shon knew that support was coming, he called me.

I will never forget that call from Shon on November 1, 2018, at 4:30 pm. He told me in a very calm voice that he had crashed and was hurt. I was confused. I didn't know that he had decided to do a couple more touch-and-goes. The last thing I'd heard was that he was going to load the plane and ride out with Ray. Shon's voice was so calm that it took me a good bit to put together what he was saying. When Shon apologized for crashing our plane, it started to sink in, but I still thought it was minor damage because he was so calm. It didn't occur to me that he could be seriously injured.

I asked how much damage there was to the plane. "It is bad," he replied. I then realized that he had been in a severe crash. I asked if he was hurt. Very calmly, he answered, "I think I broke my chest." I asked if he was bleeding, and he said he was. As soon as I realized the gravity of the situation, Shon asked me to pray. I fell to my knees in our living room and begged God to be with Shon.

I never even said "Amen" before I started asking Shon more questions about his injuries. He didn't want to talk anymore but said he wanted to try to get out of the plane. He didn't tell me that gas was leaking all around him and that he was afraid that it would catch on fire while he was trapped. We hung up the phone, and I felt utterly helpless. I prayed again for Shon and then prayed for myself. I needed to get to town. It was going to be dark soon, so I had to start figuring out a way to town so I could be there for my husband.

Rescue

It wasn't long after Shon's call to Ray that he saw the Husky circling overhead. Shon knew that he had been located. Word had gotten out that he had crashed, and several people called to check on him. The state police called and kept Shon on the line until the Pararescuemen (also known as PJs) arrived. The rescuers were in a Pave Hawk helicopter, and there was no place to land near the crash site. They had to land about a mile away and two of the rescuers hiked into the site, each carrying rescue gear. As they approached, Tom, one of the PJs, called out because he knew most pilots in Alaska were armed. He didn't want to be mistaken for a bear and shot. When they got to Shon, they took his gun and his phone and got to work.

It took them a while to assess the situation. The PJs had equipment to cut Shon out of the airplane, but because of the amount of fuel around the plane, they decided they couldn't risk a spark. They pried the door off with hand tools. Once they had an open passage, Tom told Shon that he could give him medication to knock him out, but they really needed his help pushing to extract Shon from the plane. He said it was going to suck and suck bad. Shon decided he needed to help them, so he told them, "Let's get this done!" It did hurt, and Shon screamed in pain as they pulled him from the wreckage. The extraction from the plane took about an hour. After they got Shon out, they gave him a shot of Ketamine and put him into a litter, wrapping him up like a cocoon. His face was all that was exposed. Shon had been involved in lots of rescue missions. This was the only time he had ever been the one needing rescued.

The cottonwood trees in the area were about 100 feet tall. The helicopter hovered right above the tree line, and they used 120 feet of cable to extract Shon and Tom from the scene. The wind started blowing during the hoist, so the other rescuer had to hike back to the original landing site with about ninety pounds of gear. The helicopter picked him up, and they all headed to Providence Hospital in Anchorage. On the thirty-minute flight, Shon experienced some freaky hallucinations. He described them later as dark kaleidoscopes of color and sound. Tom told Shon several times that he was going to be okay, but at one point, Shon thought he was dead because of the odd visions he was having. He finally decided that he couldn't be dead because he hurt too much.

When they landed at the helipad at the hospital, the Ketamine was starting to wear off. They put Shon on a gurney and rolled him into the hospital. There were about ten doctors and nurses around him, and they started running him down the hall, just like in the movies. He thought for sure he was going to die at that point. There was a woman who kept pushing on his sternum. Every time she did, he would scream. After about the third or fourth time, Shon looked over and asked her, "What the hell are you doing?" She looked stunned and someone else told her to quit.

Shon was in excruciating pain. There was a lot of what happened that he doesn't remember, but he did remember the CT scan. The technician told Shon that he needed to put his arms over his head. Shon looked at him like he was crazy, but the guy assured him that it was necessary. Shon screamed once more as he hoisted his arms up over his head so they could find out how bad things were. After the CT scan, a nurse came in and told him that I was on the way and would be getting there in about thirty minutes. He asked her to get him cleaned up so the blood wouldn't scare me when I got there.

Getting to Town

When I got that call from Shon, I was stunned. Even though I have received lots of emergency phone calls over the years about my husband, I wasn't prepared to get this one. We had been through twenty-eight years in law enforcement with not one single trip to the emergency room. He had been in gun battles without a scratch. How could he be hurt now that we were retired and having so much fun? It didn't feel real. I didn't know if anyone was on their way to help him, so I called Johnny. Johnny was a retired Alaska State Trooper and pilot. I knew he would know just who to call to get Shon some help. I called him first. He got the essential information and told me he would start getting help on the way.

I knew I needed to get as many people to pray for Shon as I could. I called Shon's mom first to tell her that Shon was hurt and needed prayer. I called my boys. Kyle had been deployed to UAE that week and I knew he would be asleep. Jared was working in the oil field in Texas. Both boys started praying and offered to come to Alaska to be with me. I told them to wait until we knew more. I called my older brother so he could contact the rest of my family. I called my friend Kay. She was shocked to find out Shon had crashed after I had asked her to pray for his safety just minutes before. I called Shon back to see how he was doing. He said he was still trying to get out of the plane and couldn't talk.

I called Riska to find out what they knew. She was very upset and said Ray was calling a friend to see if he could come get me in his helicopter. Ray was too shocked by the events to fly out to get me. I called Walt to see if he could get me into Willow. He was afraid his Maule wouldn't be able to stop on our short runway if there was any ice on it, so he asked me to check it before he headed out. I ran to the airstrip, fighting back my hysteria, and it looked like ice all over it to me. I called him back and told him not to try it. I would get to town another way. About that time, my neighbor, Roger, came over to help. He looked at the airstrip, called Walt back, and they decided Walt would give it a try. Roger started driving his Argo up and down the runway to break up the icy patches.

The Alaska State Trooper Dispatch called me while I was throwing things in a bag for my trip to town. Brittany, the dispatcher, explained what was happening on their end. She told me that they were sending the Air National Guard because they had better equipment for handling situations like ours. Brittany said to me that they had Shon on the phone, and he kept telling them to tell me that he loved me. I got mad and told her she didn't need to tell me that. In a stern voice, I informed her, "Shon already told me that he loved me." Later, I realized why it had made me angry. That's what people say when they are dying.

My phone kept blowing up with calls and texts as people started hearing about the crash. I continued to ask for prayer. I got online and asked for prayer for Shon on Facebook. When Walt arrived, I was relieved to see that he got the Maule stopped before the airstrip ran out. I was convinced he was going to crash as well. As Roger and I drove up to the airplane, we had to laugh. Walt, always practical, had made the most of his trip out. He was unloading several boxes for

Roger that he had been storing in his hangar. It was good to laugh. As I jumped in the little plane for the trip to town, I had to fight down a sudden fear of flying. I told myself that it was ridiculous and that I needed to get to town for Shon.

On the trip in, I got a text from Riska informing me that the helicopter had arrived. They were getting Shon out of the wreckage. The entire trip to Willow, Walt told me of every airplane crash story he knew. When we were coming in for the landing, Walt said what he always said when he was flying: "Ann, don't let me die!" Walt made me laugh even in the middle of this stressful situation. He refused to let me pay him for the flight, for which I will always be extremely thankful. It was a risky flight, and he did it out of the goodness of his heart.

Kay and Robert met me at the Willow Airport. I was busy answering calls and texts when Riska pulled up. We decided to drive out to Ray and Riska's house so I could get Shon's bag and our truck. Robert dropped Kay and me off at my pickup, and we headed to Anchorage, with Ray and Riska right behind us in their truck. Robert was going to meet us there. My phone continued to ring. I had offers of places to stay in Eagle River and in Anchorage. People were offering the use of vehicles. I had calls from people in the Lower Forty-eight asking if they needed to get on an airplane to come help me. Within just a couple of hours of that first call, I realized that I had more friends than I could ever imagine. Never before had I needed my friends this much.

About halfway to Anchorage, I realized that I could call the hospital to check on Shon's status. When I called, they said he was getting a CT scan, but everything looked pretty good. They thought he might have a broken arm. I asked them to tell Shon that I was on my way, and I started to relax a little bit. This might not be too bad.

N3227M

When I got to the ER, I checked in with Security. They gave me a sticker to put on and directed me to Room 3. When I came in, a woman was cleaning Shon's face, and a young man was putting a splint on Shon's left arm. A doctor introduced himself and started telling me about Shon's injuries. I still thought he just had a broken arm, so I was surprised when the doctor started out our conversation with, "There won't be any paralysis." He started telling me that there were some spinal fractures that scared me to death. He kept trying to go on with some of the other injuries, but I was stuck on the spinal fractures. He finally drew a picture for me on a paper towel and told me that they were hairline fractures and they seemed to be the least of our worries. After I got over the shock of realizing that this was much worse than just a broken arm, he continued to tell me the extent of the injuries.

Shon had a broken nose, two deep gashes in his face, a fractured sternum, nine rib fractures along his left side, a broken ulna, and his lung was punctured in three places. Later we realized that he also had a broken tooth and his left heel was fractured. I was trying hard not to pass out. I wanted to hear everything the doctor had to say. I noticed blood coming out of Shon's right eye and asked about that. I was afraid he had head injuries, but the doctor said that blood was coming from the gash along his nose. The man putting the splint on Shon's arm finally finished and another doctor came in and started stitching up the deep, five- to six-inch gash along his left jawline. It was deep, and the doctor was using a big, curved needle. I realized that the wound looked just like the handle on the window of the plane.

194

Kay, Robert, Ray, and Riska came in all together, which was such a comfort to me. Shon started making jokes, much to my surprise. Ray asked the doctor who was stitching Shon up if he could stitch up my mouth as well, which I thought was funny. At one point, the doctors ran everyone out but me. Ray, Riska, Kay, and Robert all stood in the hall, looking in. Shon started telling me how close he thought he was to dying, and I started getting light-headed again. Riska and Kay saw that I wasn't doing too well, grabbed me up, and took me to the waiting room. Robert and Ray were right behind us.

When they got me out there, they sat me down, and I started shaking all over. Ray gave me his coat, and Riska got some water for me. I turned white as a sheet. It took them a while to get me back together. When I finally quit shaking, we went back in, but they had taken Shon up to ICU, Room 227. It was late. Kay and Robert decided to head home, but Ray and Riska stayed with me. We were sent up to the waiting room where we sat and talked about what a miracle it was that Shon was still alive. Ray and Riska were amazed that his injuries were not more extensive. They stayed with me until I got the word that I could be with Shon again in ICU.

It took a while for them to get Shon settled. They had to do a chest x-ray and get a morphine drip going. When they finally came to get me, Shon was cleaned up a little better but still in excruciating pain. He couldn't move without hurting. He had on a cervical collar, and his face around the gash was swollen. They had to put in a second IV because the two medicines they were using to keep him comfortable were not compatible. It took three people, and many tries, to start another IV. He was in so much pain already, and I hated to see him in more as they searched for a good vein. He was freezing when I first came in and asked for more blankets. They brought more, and

I covered him up even better. As the medicine kicked in, he got really hot and wanted all the blankets off. Small adjustments were painful, and he groaned most of the night. At one point, a doctor came in and started talking to me about his injuries and the amount of pain he was experiencing. Again, I began to pass out and had to sit down. It was a long night.

As I sat there during the night, I knew that it was going to be a long recovery, and we wouldn't be able to make it back out to our cabin for a while. I asked God what we would do. He gently reminded me of a conversation we'd had with a nice gentleman a month or so ago. He had offered the use of his house if we ever needed it. He was going down South and told us we could use it at any time. We had thought it was a little odd when he made the offer. We had only met him a couple of times and it seemed a bit out of the ordinary.

Then God did something else for me. He said, "3227." Those numbers rolled around in my head until the next day when I finally figured it out. Our tail number on the wrecked airplane was N3227M. They had taken Shon to Room 3 in the ER and then to Room 227 in ICU. That wasn't a coincidence. It was a way for God to remind me that He was in control, no matter how bad things looked at the moment. He had even arranged a place for us to stay before we knew we needed it.

God's Protection

Over the next several days, I realized how much God had protected Shon. He was in terrible pain, but the doctors assured us that he would heal. They were genuinely surprised at how all his injuries would just need time. They didn't think he would need any surgeries. Even his broken arm was perfectly aligned. The orthopedic surgeon put a splint on Shon's arm that first night in the ER and later transitioned to a removable cast. They were watching his lung that had been punctured, but were happy that it hadn't collapsed. Everything else was left to heal on its own.

The main thing the doctors did for Shon was to help him control the pain. They put him on a morphine drip, but I had to talk Shon into pushing the button to get more medicine. He was also given opioids. Shon worried about getting addicted to the drugs, but I assured him that I would not let that happen. He had to keep the pain down so he could move around and not develop pneumonia. He was given an epidural on the second day of his stay in the hospital, which helped considerably. With the epidural, he felt good enough to get out of bed and walk. He started feeling so much better that by the third day, he decided he was better, and they could remove the epidural. He didn't think it was helping that much anyway. I'd had an epidural and knew how effective they were at blocking pain. I was flabbergasted when the doctor agreed to remove the epidural. She said she would stop the medicine early the next morning and they would check in on Shon throughout the day to see if he wanted them to start it back up. If he was still doing okay by noon, they would remove the epidural and he could get his first shower.

I thought they were both crazy but neither of them would listen to me. Shon was almost giddy about his brush with death and miraculous survival. One of the nurses told him he was "Miracle Boy," and he embraced his new nickname. By noon the next day, Shon was still convinced that he was fine. The opioids seemed to be keeping the pain down, and he wanted that shower.

After the nurse removed the port for the epidural, it was time to get Shon cleaned up. The nurses agreed to let me help Shon in the shower. I had not seen the injuries to his left side that were hidden by the hospital gown. I had been focusing on his arm and the gashes to his face. I knew he had broken ribs and sternum, but I was not prepared for the massive amount of bruises that covered his entire left side from his thigh up to his shoulder. As I helped him get into the shower, I had to stop for a moment while I sobbed. Poor Shon comforted me while standing there, dripping wet with all the medical tubing tangled around us. I finally got myself together, thanking God for His protection, and we finished getting Shon his much-needed shower.

That evening we had visitors. Kay and Robert had driven over to check on us. They couldn't believe how much better Shon looked. We all talked and laughed for about half an hour when I realized that Shon had quit talking. I looked over at Shon. His happy attitude that had been so prevalent over the last couple of days was gone. I interrupted the conversation to ask Shon if he was okay. He looked at me and said, "The epidural just wore off."

Shon was in the hospital for five days. I was nervous when they cut us loose. I didn't think I was prepared to deal with the extensive injuries, but they booted us out of the door anyway. Shon was more than ready to leave. While we were on our way out, he said to me, "Honey, I cheated death one more time!" I didn't appreciate his humor.

Yea, though I walk through the valley of the shadow of death, I will fear no evil; For thou art with me; Your rod and Your staff, they comfort me.

Psalm 23:4 KJV

CHAPTER 10

Recovery

Fishing Joe and Vicki

Our good friend, Fishing Joe, and his wife, Vicki, called me as soon as they heard about the accident. They graciously offered me a place to stay while Shon was in the hospital in Anchorage. I stayed with Shon every night during his time in the hospital, but went to their house to shower. They were so sweet to ask about Shon's recovery and listened as I went over each detail. It was comforting for me to have someone to talk to about the situation. I found it somewhat ironic that it was Fishing Joe that God sent to listen to me.

I was a nervous wreck when the doctors dismissed Shon from the hospital. He was still on several pain killers, and I was afraid I was going to mix them up. Everything Shon did was a struggle. He couldn't even put on his clothes by himself. I wasn't even sure he could climb into our truck. I didn't want to leave the safety of the doctors and nurses. Fishing Joe and Vicki knew I was concerned and asked us to stay at their house in Anchorage until I felt better about Shon's condition.

When we got to Fishing Joe's house that night after leaving the hospital, Vicki had a meal ready for us when we walked into the house. I hated feeling like we were intruding, but their kindness quickly put me at ease. In just a bit, Fishing Joe started telling airplane crash jokes and had us all laughing. Shon held a pillow up to his sternum while he laughed to keep it from hurting too much. Finally, Shon told him he had to stop joking. The laughing hurt too much.

We stayed with them for two days, Shon sleeping each night in Joe's recliner. I kept track of the medications on a notepad so I wouldn't give him too much or too little. We went each day to stores so Shon could walk. The doctors told us he needed to get up and exercise as much as possible to prevent pneumonia. Shon looked pitiful. He wore an oversized shirt and huge coat that I'd bought at a thrift store that would go over the splint on his arm. Instead of his regular pants, he wore warmups due to the swelling along his left side. I'd bought him some slip-on shoes to make my life easier. And then there was the deep gash along his jaw and his nose. He looked rough. He was shuffling along at one store when a lady came up and said, "Oh, look at you, getting your exercise," like he was 100 years old. When she walked away, he asked, "Do I look that bad?" I hated to tell him that he did.

Recovering the Plane

There have been quite a few small airplanes crash in Alaska over the years. They even have a law that states that a person who crashes a plane is responsible for cleaning up the crash site. No need to let all of those smashed airplanes litter up the place. I didn't know about that law, and the wreckage was the least of my worries. Shon knew it was our responsibility but was in no shape to do anything about it. Shon was still in ICU when Johnny and Ray started talking about how to get the plane out of its resting spot. It was in a hard place to reach. The temperature was dipping below zero at times, but the river hadn't frozen over yet. The only way to get the plane out was by helicopter.

Johnny arranged for some of his neighborhood friends to land a Super Cub on a gravel bar not too far from the crash site. They hiked to the plane in the subzero weather and cut the airplane into four pieces with a cordless reciprocating saw. About a week and a half after the accident, Johnny called to let us know that Mike and his wife, Jayne, had arranged for a helicopter to hoist the wreckage over to Ray's airstrip. Johnny picked us up at FBI Billy's house, and we drove to Willow to watch.

It was a sad, gray day. I could tell Shon was in severe pain, made worse by the single-digit temperature. There were several people at Ray's to help with the process, most of whom I didn't know. Shon had met some of them at Johnny's house at one time or another. We drove to the end of the bluff when the Robinson R-44 helicopter arrived and watched as it disappeared into the trees in that horrible spot. After a few minutes, the R-44 flew past us with the first load. They had tied the two wings together, and they were catching a lot of wind as they went by us. We loaded back into the truck and drove up the runway. We watched as they slowly lowered them to a clearing next to the airstrip. A person on the ground released the wings so the R-44 could go back for another load. They made two more trips, once to get the motor, and once to get the fuselage.

I knew it was going to be hard seeing the wreckage, but it was worse than I thought. I saw a dent in the wing where Shon had hit the cottonwood tree, bringing him to an instant stop. It was huge. The propeller was bent terribly, even though I knew it hadn't been spinning when he hit the ground. But what got me the most was the inside of the cockpit. There was blood all over it. Johnny picked up the seat cushion to look at the condition of the pilot's seat. The seat that I'd been looking forward to sitting in was demolished. I saw the broken tubing and crushed plywood, gaining a better understanding of the severity of the impact. The left side of the cockpit bulged out. It was apparent Shon's body had hit down and to the left. The throttle was bent, as was the window frame where Shon's arm would have been during the ordeal. Looking at the cockpit, it hit us all how close Shon came to death.

Picture of N3227M at the crash site, November of 2018

Picture of N3227M at the crash site, November of 2018

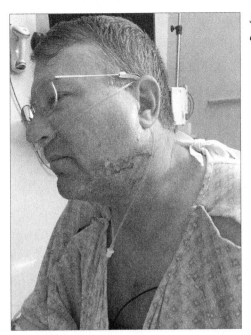

Shon in the hospital after the crash, November of 2018

Recovering the airplane, November of 2018

Recovering the airplane, November of 2018

Shon lost one of his hearing aids during the crash, so Ray and I looked in the airplane to see if we could find it. After a bit, Ray found it in the smashed headset, surprising us all. After that, I pulled items from the plane. I grabbed the pack of required survival gear for winter flying. Shon laughed and said, "I've always heard that you can't count on any survival gear that is not on your person. That is so true. I could have used the wool blanket, but there was no way I could reach it in the condition I was in at the time of the crash."

By this time, a small crowd had gathered around the plane. The mood was somber. I heard a few people tell Shon that they sure were sorry about the accident. In just a little while, these people I didn't know were telling us their stories of wrecked airplanes, injuries, and how they'd survived. I could tell that their stories were making Shon feel better. It was brutally cold, but their love and support warmed my heart.

I saw that the helicopter crew was getting ready to go, so I ran to get my checkbook. I wasn't sure how much it was going to cost, but I thought I'd heard an estimate of a thousand dollars. When I asked for the amount, the young man said that someone had already taken care of the expense, and we didn't owe a thing. Shon and I were completely overwhelmed.

Fluid Removal and Peanut Butter Pie

I could never be a doctor or a nurse. I pass out at the sight of blood and don't do well in emergencies. I have very little mercy for people in pain and struggle with patience. Here I was, suddenly thrust into the role of the primary caregiver to an airplane crash victim. Not only was I washing Shon's pants, but I also had to put them on him. He needed help showering and merely getting out of a chair. I kept up with his medication and doctor appointments. I did all of the driving. I dropped Shon off at the front door everywhere we went so he wouldn't slip on the ice in the parking lots. I would love to say that I relished my new role, but I can't. It was *hard*.

Three weeks after the accident, Shon had a follow-up appointment with the trauma team. I was frustrated because we never saw the same doctor. This group of doctors focused on the internal injuries around Shon's broken ribs and sternum. I knew Shon had a punctured lung, but it hadn't collapsed. In the hospital, all I heard these doctors say was that there wasn't much they could do for the ribs and sternum. They would heal on their own. I almost canceled the appointment because I figured we would hear more of the same. When I called to cancel, I asked why we needed to come in for a follow-up visit. The person I talked to couldn't answer my question, but she did tell me they were going to do a chest x-ray. Hearing that, I decided it was worth the drive to Anchorage on the icy roads.

It was the day before Thanksgiving when we drove in for Shon's appointment. Shon got the x-ray, and then we headed upstairs to get the results. We were surprised when the doctor said we needed another CT scan after looking at the x-ray. She explained that there had been fluid around Shon's lungs while he was in the hospital, and the x-ray determined if it was increasing or decreasing. She said that there appeared to be more fluid than before, surprising both Shon and me. We needed the CT scan to be sure. She scheduled the scan in Wasilla for later that afternoon. After we had the scan done, they told us at the imaging center that they would have someone call us that day if there was a problem. If there were no issues, they would give us a call with the results on Monday, after the Thanksgiving weekend. When we didn't hear anything that day, we were cautiously hopeful. But I knew how busy everyone was right before a holiday weekend.

The next day, we had Thanksgiving lunch with Kay and Robert and then spent time that afternoon with Ray and Riska. On Saturday night, we went to a post-Thanksgiving party at Mike and Jayne's hangar. Everyone brought leftovers. Many of the guys that had helped with the recovery of the airplane were there with guitars. There was even an electric piano set up under the wing of Mike's Skywagon. I thoroughly enjoyed the evening singing hymns and getting to know people from the Meadow Lakes neighborhood. Shon was in pain but enjoyed being out of the house. Johnny's wife, Barbi, an ER nurse, asked Shon how he was doing. He mentioned the CT scan and the fluid. She told him that she hoped that fluid was gone. She explained the procedure to remove it, and it sounded horrible. I reassured Shon that they would have called if anything was wrong, but we both had a feeling that wasn't the case.

First thing Monday morning, I called the doctor's office. They were surprised that we didn't know Shon was scheduled for a procedure at one p.m. the next day. I felt so sorry for Shon. He was getting a root canal later that morning and then had the fluid removal to look forward to on the following day. I was on sympathy overload.

I left Shon at the hospital for the procedure. There wasn't a thing I could do to help, and I was about to go bonkers. I called a friend I'd met out in the bush who also had a house in town, and she came to pick me up. Shon was going to call me when he was finished, in an hour or so. Robin and I went to a little coffee shop that she liked and ordered some pie and coffee, settling in for a short visit. The waitress brought out the piece of peanut butter pie I'd ordered. It was huge, and it was *rich*. After just a few bites, I had to put down my fork.

We were there for three hours. The longer we were there, the more I worried about Shon. I found myself taking bite after bite of the pie. By the time my phone rang, my plate was empty, and I was *miserable*.

Robin took me back to the hospital, where we found Shon sitting on a bench. He looked horrible. Shon told us about the ordeal.

When he went in, he removed his shirt and leaned over a tray table with his arms over his head. One woman was there to do a sonogram to identify where the incision needed to be. The other woman used that information to cut a hole in Shon's upper back and insert a tube. She pushed the tubing in through his back, between his ribs, and attempted to get it below his lungs. For whatever reason, they were unable to get any fluid out.

While they were fishing around, Shon got sick and told them that he was going to pass out. They yanked the tube out and let him lay back for a few minutes until his nausea passed. They called in another doctor to help the second time around. They used the sonogram again while they inserted the tube, to make sure it went to the correct spot. They were successful and sucked out 500 ml of fluid. Shon said it looked like Pilsner beer. He reiterated that the entire procedure was just awful.

I felt for the guy, I really did, but I was pretty darn miserable myself. That pie seemed to be growing. I had to keep sitting up straight, giving it more room to expand. I took deep breaths. Shon finally realized that I seemed to be in some pain and asked what was wrong. He didn't seem sympathetic to my situation at all as I told of my harrowing pie-eating experience and my current suffering. I may not be a very good nurse, but he had no mercy for me whatsoever.

7.1 Earthquake of 2018

As the morning dawned on the last day of November, Shon and I woke up thankful he was on the mend. Even though he was still in pain, his ribs and sternum were growing back nicely. His arm was in a removable cast, and all of the swelling was subsiding. He was even wearing his regular clothes and shoes again. Since Shon was doing better, Kay and I had plans to meet up that day for some Christmas shopping.

Shon and I were in the guest room of FBI Billy's house getting ready for the day when we heard a rumble. In just a few seconds, Shon and I both felt the house start to shake. I recognized that we were experiencing an earthquake. Typically, they only last a few seconds. This one kept going. At one point, it felt like the house was riding a massive wave. I heard glasses breaking in the kitchen. A television in the guest room fell over, but Shon caught it with his good arm. As the shaking continued, all of the lights went out, and we found ourselves in the dark. We stayed right where we were until the earthquake subsided. I was freaking out a bit, but Shon was calm, cool, and collected, as always.

Something happened at that moment. There was a shift in the roles between Shon and me. I had been caring for him nonstop for a month and had been protecting him from anything that might bring him harm. When the earthquake started shaking that day, he became my protector once again. He still had injuries, but I looked to him for strength. As the ground shook beneath us, Shon reassured me that everything was going to be okay.

When the floors quit moving, we went to investigate the damage. I thought for sure that the house was going to break into several pieces, but it was still standing. The kitchen was full of broken glass, and many of the pictures were hanging at weird angles. A plant had tipped over. We found a few more little things broken throughout the house.

Shon and I headed to the attached hangar to check on things there. We opened the utility room to check on the gas and water lines. Everything seemed okay. We were walking back through the hangar when the first aftershock hit. Here we were in this massive room with animal mounts hanging all around the perimeter of the ceiling. Billy's airplane, a PA-14 on floats, was hanging from the ceiling. The aftershock was scarier than the first wave. The aircraft swung around wildly and tools fell from their places along the walls. Shon hollered at me, "Let's get out of here!" I ran, and he shuffled back into the house. Over the next half hour or so, we had several more aftershocks.

When things seemed to calm down, I inspected the outside of the house and foundation for any cracks. It was perfect. We had no electricity, and the house was getting cold quickly. Shon and I figured it might be days before we had any service, so he lit a small gas stove in one part of the house so we could have some heat. We finally made our way back to the hangar and found that one of the enormous caribou mounts had fallen and busted. I was so glad we hadn't been under that thing when it came down from the wall. It didn't take us long to clean up the messes.

After we knew that things were okay at Billy's house, we gave our neighbor on Cub Lake, Roger, a call. We had no idea how the earthquake had affected him, and we were concerned about our cabin and dog as well. Roger was okay, as was our sweet pup, Kuma. Roger told us that Kuma had been plenty concerned during the ordeal. Roger said he would call us back after he went across the lake to check out how our house had fared.

We were relieved to hear later that our house had no damage at all. No dishes had even come out of the cabinets. The only thing

Roger found broken was a small figurine of a woman that I kept on a window sill. She was on the floor. Bob and Ruth had done a great job building our cabin. I was so thankful for their hard work and the strong foundation they had laid.

It didn't take us long to realize that our cabin at Cub Lake and FBI Billy's house had done better than most in the surrounding area. Even though it was freezing outside, people were coming out of their homes to check on their neighbors. As with most disasters, people in the neighborhood came together to seek comfort and provide support for one another.

In less than two hours, we were shocked when the lights came back on and we had electricity once again. We turned on the television and found that many roads were damaged. Schools were closed, and people were being sent home from work. Pictures of the damage at grocery stores started popping up on my newsfeed on Facebook. Hardware stores had spilled paint in the aisles, along with fallen merchandise. I saw a picture of a car that had been on a road that had collapsed all around it. There was a picture that was circulating of children on Vine Road. The roadway had a massive crater in it, with kids climbing in the debris. The local television stations had continuous coverage of the earthquake, with government officials giving updates about roads shut down for repairs. We also listened for news of any deaths. This earthquake was the same magnitude as the one in Haiti that had killed 200,000 people. Thankfully, there were no deaths reported due to this shaker.

I was glad we had plenty of groceries on hand. I didn't know how long it would be before the stores were open for business. Shon had a doctor's appointment in Anchorage in a couple of days, which I thought would be impossible to make. Shon and I figured it would take a good while for the roads to open. Boy, were we wrong. The Alaskan spirit was alive and well, and the road workers were busy fixing the damage immediately. They worked day and night, allowing people to travel freely in a couple of days. We made our appointment in Anchorage two days later, driving over many of the damaged spots that we had seen in the news. I was amazed and very impressed with the Alaskan Department of Transportation.

Everywhere we went, strangers wanted to share their stories with us. People were drawn together in the shared traumatic experience. It hit me once again that there is healing in the telling. "Where were you? What damage did you have?" People we talked to were concerned about their pets who had been traumatized by the shaking and falling debris. Some were dealing with water wells that suffered damage in the quake. We continued to have aftershocks each day. It became a game for most Alaskans to guess the magnitude of the last shaker and then check it against the newly installed earthquake apps we had on our phones, to see how close we were.

The first day of November was the crash, and the last day of the month was the earthquake. November was officially my least favorite month. I informed Shon that he could no longer use his "I was in an airplane crash" card. I was *done*.

The Love of a Neighbor

From the time I found out that Shon had crashed, our neighbor and friend, Roger, was there to help. Not only did he make sure I got to town the night of the accident, but he also took care of our place the two months we were in town. He told us not to worry about anything out at Cub Lake. We knew our cabin, our precious Kuma dog, and my flock of chickens were being tended to by Roger. He made the trek to the house twice a day to put wood in the stove, feeding the chickens on the morning run over. He gathered eggs, kept an eye on our batteries, and even watered my plants. Kuma didn't like being alone at our cabin, so Roger invited him to stay over at his place. We will forever be thankful for the kindness of our neighbor and friend.

Who Needs Enemies?

Our friends in town were good about checking on us and made sure we got out of the house from time to time. After being in town for a month, Ray and Riska invited us to eat breakfast with them one Sunday morning before church. They told us to meet them at the restaurant at Deshka Landing, Eaglequest, so we got up early and headed over for a visit. When we walked in, Ray and Riska were there with another couple we had met. I thought they all looked like they were up to something, but I couldn't figure out what it was.

We all ordered and were visiting when Kevin, the owner, came over with a bucket and sign, presenting it to me with much fanfare. It was a beggar's sign asking for donations. They portrayed me as a woman with a banged-up husband and a wrecked airplane. They had passed the bucket around before we had arrived and had gathered up a whopping seventeen cents. One guy hadn't wanted to cough up any money, so he had written a note suggesting how *not* to crash. Riska took a picture of me holding up my sign and bucket while everyone there laughed. Ray then informed Shon that he was no longer qualified to be called an Alaskan bush pilot. The pilots in the area had renamed him an Alaskan "tree pilot" since he'd landed in the trees. It was good to finally get to the point where we could laugh about it, but it did make me consider: Who needs enemies when we have friends like these?

Ann with her Begging Bucket, December of 2018

Yearning for Home

FBI Billy's house was beautiful, and I enjoyed having a dishwasher to use. Being in town made life more convenient, but Shon and I missed our cabin on Cub Lake. It was getting close to Christmas, and we found ourselves yearning for our home. We missed the view of the lake and the solitude. But more than anything, we missed Kuma. We knew he had to be wondering what had happened to us. When the doctors finally thought Shon was doing well enough to travel, we arranged a flight back home.

Kevin was a pilot who lived in the Meadow Lakes neighborhood. He had a four-place 185 on skis and offered to fly us home five days before Christmas. He knew that it was Shon's first flight after the accident and sensed that Shon was a little nervous about it. We packed up our belongings and groceries, and took off, headed for home. When we got about halfway, we ran into a thick wall of fog, forcing us to turn back. Kevin knew how much we wanted to get home. He was apologetic, but we assured him that it was okay. We would make it when the weather cleared.

When we got back over the runway, Kevin lined us up and landed the plane. The landing was bumpy, to put it mildly. We bounced all over the place. Kevin, feeling even worse about the bumps, looked at Shon and said, "That was your first landing since….(he didn't want to say *the crash*)… your last landing." I laughed and replied, "That would be true for all of us, now wouldn't it?" Kevin rolled his eyes at me, and we decided to try again in a couple of days.

The weather was cold and clear two days later when we attempted the trip home once again. The flight out was beautiful, flying over snow-covered terrain that was becoming quite familiar to us. I recognized landmarks as we got closer to Cub Lake. Roger had packed down a runway on the back lake to provide a more extended place to land the 185. Kevin landed it perfectly and Roger was there to meet us. We unpacked our supplies into our plastic tub and thanked Kevin for the ride. As he took off over us, he waggled his wings and made the turn back to town.

I was concerned about Shon riding the snow machine, but it didn't seem to bother him much as we made the half-mile trip home. As we rode around the corner, our cabin came into view. It looked so inviting. And then we saw Kuma. Shon yelled, "Come here, boy!" Kuma's eyes lit up, and he came running to us as fast as he could. He seemed to sense that Shon was hurt and did not jump up on him or play with him rough like he usually did. Kuma ran from Shon to me, as excited as I had ever seen him. After he'd settled down a bit, he followed us home, happy to have us all back together. It was so good to be home, and just in time for Christmas.

Christmas with Ray, Riska, and Roger at the Cabin
on Cub Lake, December of 2018

Shoveling Snow

It snowed significantly more at Cub Lake than it had in town. Shon became concerned about the weight of the snow on our roof. It was about three feet thick, and Shon had never let it pile up that much before. There was no way he was climbing up on our two-story house to shovel snow in his condition. My patience as a nurse had long run dry, and I didn't want him to take the chance of injuring himself. If anyone was going to fall off of the roof and need to be waited on hand and foot, I wanted it to be me. Reluctantly, Shon agreed to me climbing up the ladder and shoveling the snow.

Roger must have seen me on the roof from his cabin and felt sorry for me. Before long, he was on the roof, helping me remove the heavy snow. I never knew what a difficult of a job it was. My arms quickly turned to jelly. When my arms couldn't shovel anymore, I developed another technique. I used my shovel to cut out a block of snow about a foot square and then pushed it slowly over the edge of the roof onto the growing piles of snow below. That worked for a while until I accidentally pushed my shovel off of the roof with the snow. I had to climb down the ladder, trudge through the extra-deep snow, and retrieve my shovel. Roger and I worked until we were exhausted. I thanked him for his help and told him I would finish it the next morning.

Even though my arms were sore, I climbed back up the ladder the next day to continue my work. As I fought to rid the roof of the heavy snow, I had several thoughts. First, I *never* wanted to start a snow-removal business. No matter how much money they made, it wasn't worth it. Second, I had to pay attention to what I was doing. When we had cloud cover, the snow blended in with that on the ground, making it all look flat. There were a couple of times I found myself dangerously close to the edge. Third, I remembered being critical of Shon's snow removal in the past. When it snowed, the roof looked like a nicely decorated cake with fluffy. white frosting. I loved taking pictures of the cabin like that. When Shon shoveled the snow off, it was uneven and didn't look nearly as picturesque. Had I asked him to even it out to make it pretty? Surely I hadn't. And if I did, I owed him a huge apology.

Timber!

In the past, Shon and I had gotten our wood supply in February and March while we could get around on the snow machines. We weren't sure how we were going to do it with Shon's injuries but decided we needed to do what we could. When we had been home for about a month, I asked him to go with me to find some trees to pack around. I found some skinny trees, ones that were not too intimidating, and Shon watched as I rode his snow machine, "The Beast," around and around to create a hard surface, just as he instructed. The next day, we prepared for the scariest part. It was the day we would see if I could fell a tree. Kuma was so excited as we warmed up the snow machines, and Shon got the chainsaws out. It was like he knew things were getting back to "normal."

I was anxious when we got to my skinny tree and I was the one holding the chainsaw instead of my husband. Shon was so sweet. He stood behind me and gave very detailed instructions, using his hand to show me the angle of the cuts I needed to make. I made two cuts on the front of the tree. Shon was excited to see that I had successfully cut a wedge and he proudly removed it from the tree. We moved back to the other side, and I started with the horizontal cut from the backside, watching to make sure Kuma was out of the path of the tree. It didn't take long for the tree to start to wobble, and then down it went. The small birch didn't make the ground shake like Shon's big trees, but it was a sight. I couldn't think of the word "*Timber!*" in my excitement, but I let out a big whoop.

The tree landed precisely where I wanted it to go. I limbed it out as Shon pulled away the smaller limbs. I cut the tree into two manageable pieces. We muscled the two logs onto a contraption called a "log bump," which is a small sled with skis. The log bump lifted the front ends of the logs off of the ground to make them drag easily behind the snow machine. We pulled the two logs over to the wood splitter that Ken had freighted out for us. I was thrilled to get that first tree to the house, knowing that we were going to be able to get our wood in before spring.

Ray, Mr. Nice Guy

Ray liked to act tough. He even enjoyed giving Shon a hard time about being a "tree pilot" instead of a bush pilot, but I'd seen Ray the night of the crash. Ray was a mess that night. He hated the fact that Shon had crashed and did everything he could do to help us get back on our feet.

After we got back home, Ray called almost every day, checking on Shon and talking about airplanes. I didn't know men could yap so much about a single subject, but they did. (And still do.) Even though the NTSB had done an investigation into the crash, there were no answers as to why the engine failed that fateful day. Many of their conversations revolved around what had caused the crash. I could tell he was also encouraging Shon to get back into flying. Shon and I had decided in the hospital on Day Two that we weren't going to let this crash keep us from flying, but I knew it was going to be difficult for Shon to climb into the pilot's seat that first time. Ray surprised us both when he asked Shon if he thought he was ready to fly again. My ears perked up as I listened for Shon's reply. "Yes, I'm ready," he said. Ray told him that he would fly out the next day to pick Shon up in his Husky.

When Shon got off the phone, I asked him what Ray meant. Shon wasn't sure if Ray meant that they would fly around with Shon in the back. Maybe he intended for Shon to fly with the controls in the back seat. Shon wasn't sure what to expect. He did know, however, that Ray had *never, ever* let anyone fly his plane.

True to his word, Ray flew out the next day and landed on Cub Lake. Like I've said before, Shon doesn't show much emotion, but I sensed that he was nervous and excited, even though nobody else could see it. I went out on the lake with Shon, surprised at the nervousness that was creeping into my heart. Shon kissed me goodbye and crawled into the back seat. Off they went, headed back the same way Ray had come.

As they flew back towards Willow, Ray talked to Shon about flying on skis. Shon hadn't had the chance to fly our plane on skis before it had crashed. In about half an hour, Ray landed his Husky at the Willow Airport. He put a set of controls in the backseat and told Shon to take the controls in the front. Shon took off, enjoying the climb out at full throttle. After a few minutes, Ray gently reminded Shon that he could throttle back at any time. Shon hadn't even realized that he was still at full throttle, climbing like nobody's business.

Shon laughed, realizing that pulling back that throttle was making him nervous. He told Ray, "I don't want to. The last time I did that, I crashed." They laughed about it as Shon gently pulled back to cruise RPM's and made the turn in the traffic pattern. Shon had made three or four landings when Ray told him that he was bored sitting in the back seat and wanted out. Shon came to a full stop and let Ray out so he could visit with all of his old pilot buddies. Shon made several more trips in the pattern before picking Ray back up and flying home.

All of that flying took several hours. I was a nervous wreck by the time they returned, but my anxiety faded when I saw Shon's face. I could tell that he'd had a blast. And Ray looked plumb pleased with himself. I knew that the next time Ray called, he and Shon would be talking about what airplanes they had seen for sale. Within three months, they found our next bird.

May the Lord make your love increase and overflow for each other and for everyone else, just as ours does for you.

1 Thessalonians 3:12 NIV

CHAPTER 11

Let's Try This Again

Helicopter Landing

Our son, Kyle, was in the Middle East on another deployment when Shon crashed. His sweet wife, Mirai, and our new grandbaby, Russell, had planned on coming to stay with us for a few months after we returned to Cub Lake. They were to arrive in the middle of April and remain until Kyle's deployment ended, later that summer. Shon was healing nicely, but looking forward to our grandbaby's visit did wonders for us both. We counted the days until his arrival. As the time grew closer, however, we realized the weather was not going to cooperate with us.

The Alaskan Bush has four seasons: Winter, Break-Up, Summer, and Freeze-Up. Break-Up is when all of the ice melts. The lakes and rivers break up, making traveling by snow machine impossible (unless, of course, you are Ken Lee). But even he has to eventually put away his winter machine and break out the boat. And there is a time when an airplane cannot land on our lake with skis or floats because of the thin, rotting ice chunks. This year, Break-Up came early.

By the end of March, we knew that our lake was going to be in no shape for landing an airplane with Mirai and Russell. We had the 550-foot airstrip, but it still had too much snow on it for a safe landing. We were going to have to rent a helicopter for their ride out. Shon got on the phone and called the guys with the R-44 who had pulled out Blue from the trees in the Susitna River and arranged a flight.

Mirai and Russell had a long trip from Japan. She was exhausted when they landed in Anchorage. Traveling with a thirteen-month-old baby is never fun, but Russell had done relatively well on the thirteen-hour flight. Shon and I couldn't go in to meet them, but Kay and Robert offered to pick them up for us. Robert even made a sign to hold up so Mirai would know who he was when she got off of the flight. He was there waiting on them and took them back to stay the night with him and Kay at their place in Wasilla. The next morning, Kay took Mirai and Russell to the helicopter at the Wasilla Airport and saw them off.

I was so excited when we heard the helicopter approaching. The R-44 landed right in our front yard, and I could see Russell's little face through the front bubble. He looked like he was enjoying himself. Mirai and Russell got out and came over to me while Shon unloaded their gear with the rotor blades kicking up the snow. In just a few minutes, the helicopter was lifting off, heading over to pick up a backhaul from across the river.

I had Mirai back! We could play Scrabble and drink tea again. And I had my sweet grandson here for a few months. Life couldn't get much better.

Mirai and Russell getting into the helicopter, April of 2019
Photo Credit: Kay Kibbe

Introducing N2467M

During the first week of May, when the snow melted, and the ice on the lake disappeared, Ray showed up with his Husky on floats to take Shon to town to buy another PA-12. Shon had located one for sale in Wasilla that was very similar to Blue. This one was a pretty red and white plane with extended landing gear, making the nose point even higher in the air than Blue. The engine was new and had more horse-power than the last one. Robert did a pre-buy inspection as another mechanic did the annual, making sure that everything was up-to-date and in good working order.

Shon bought the plane over the phone with the owner in Oregon. All he needed to do was go to town and pick up our new ride. Red, on wheels, was parked at the mechanic's house. Shon taxied the airplane from the mechanic's driveway down a public street about a block to a grass strip in the neighborhood. Shon took off of that little strip and flew the plane to the Willow Airport, where he, Ray, and Robert spent several days working on the transition from wheels to floats. When they got it finished, Ray came out to get me so I could fly home with Shon in our new 1947 PA-12. We were ready to try this again.

Shon and Ann with N2467M, May of 2019, Photo Credit: Roger Bickleman

Russell in Alaska

After we brought the new plane home and Shon had time to fly it a few hours, he asked Mirai if she and Russell wanted to go for a flight-seeing tour of the area. I wasn't sure how she would feel about flying with Shon after his crash, especially with Russell, but she was game. Russell wasn't sure what was going on when Mirai put some ear protection on his ears and belted him in the back seat of the plane next to her. Shon climbed in the pilot's seat, and they were off.

When they took off of the lake and had some altitude, Shon looked back to see how Russell was doing. What he saw made his

Russell with his grandpa, Summer of 2019

Mirai and Russell ready to take a flight in Red, N2467M, Summer of 2019

heart soar. Russell had both hands and his face pressed up against the plexiglass door, looking out at the scenery below. He loved it!

After that first flight, Shon couldn't even check on the airplane without Russell running after him with his arms raised. When Shon picked him up near the PA-12, Russell would turn to Mirai and me and wave goodbye. He was ready to fly. Russell took many flying trips that summer and loved every one of them. I may be wrong, but I think we may have a future pilot in the Parker family.

The time with Mirai and Russell was precious, but seeing them reunited with our son, Kyle, after a long deployment in the Middle East, was even better. Families belong together, and that little boy needed his daddy.

Not Again

I could feel the anxiety start to build the closer we got to the first anniversary of the crash. As the temperatures dropped, the feelings that surrounded that horrible day closed in around Shon and me. It felt like it was going to happen again. We tried to shake the mood, but as the days drew nearer to November first, the sense of dread grew. Instead of Shon going into town by himself to make the change from floats to wheels like he had done the year before, we decided to make the trip together.

Shon watched the weather each day. He saw that we were going to get into some freezing temperatures around the middle of October. We had to get the airplane out of our lake before the water started turning to ice, so he made the appropriate arrangements in Willow. We flew in and landed on Willow Lake. A mechanic pulled us out of the lake, putting the plane on a trailer he had made for that job. He hauled Red across the street to the Willow Airport to a hangar that we had rented for the day. Ray and Robert met us there, and we all worked together to take the floats off and put the wheels on the airplane with no problems.

Here we were again. Shon had to fly the plane on wheels, just like when he crashed. As much as we were trying to change things up, the sense of dread remained. Shon had taught himself, years ago, to put unwelcome feelings away so he could deal with the job at hand and was doing just that. I had never mastered that skill, and the emotions seemed to be crushing me. They hit me especially hard when Shon taxied the airplane to the runway and took off for a few trips in the pattern. I stood in the cold, biting wind watching him take off and land, praying the entire time. I felt silly, knowing that this was the same plane that I had trusted on the trip into town. The only difference was the wheels. He finally nosed the plane towards Ray's runway. I got in the truck to meet him there. In just a few minutes, Shon was safely on the ground.

The next day, I got in the airplane with Shon. The sense of dread overtook me as we took off of the bluff and flew directly over the crash site from the year before. I looked down, amazed at the size of the cottonwood trees and the miracle of Shon's survival. We flew for two hours, making several touch-and-goes at the Willow Airport. With each successful landing, my sense of dread slowly left me. By the time we made it back to Ray's, I was feeling confident in the plane once again.

Muddy Tires

In Alaska aviation, landing on gravel bars is a way of life. Because we had been on floats, it was a type of flying that we had been unable to explore. Many pilots use gravel bars located along the river banks or in the middle of the rivers as runways. It is best to have oversized tires, because the gravel bars are full of big rocks and aren't as smooth as one might think. Other areas are sandy and can be soft. Our thirty-one-inch bush wheels also gave the propeller more clearance from the ground. Since we were on tires, Ray suggested we make a gravel bar landing.

Ray went through the process with Shon before we attempted this next type of landing. First, we had to find a gravel bar that was long enough for us to make a safe landing. When we found the right spot, we needed to make a low pass to look at the area. We needed to watch for big rocks, holes, or driftwood that might cause us problems. After visually clearing the area, we would circle the gravel bar, line up the plane, and gently set the airplane down along the strip. After discussing the process and working out the details, Shon was ready to give it a try with Ray in the lead.

I climbed in with Ray in his Husky. We took off of the bluff with Shon right behind us in the PA-12. Ray already had a gravel bar picked out that he had landed on numerous times. He made the low pass, checking the area. It looked bumpy to me. As we circled, Shon made his low pass. When Shon was out of the way, we lined up and Ray set the Husky down. We bounced a few times and came to a stop. He powered up and taxied his airplane out of Shon's way to a spot where we could see Shon's landing.

My heart was in my throat as Shon came in low. He put the plane down perfectly, like he'd been making gravel bar landings for years. He, too, powered up and swung our plane around to park right next to the Husky. I let out a sigh of relief, and we all climbed out of the airplanes, stepping out onto the muddy gravel bar.

Gravel Bar Landing, Fall of 2019

While Shon and Ray talked about the landing, I had the best time exploring the gravel bar. I found more beaver-chewed wood than I could carry. There were cool rocks and gorgeous pieces of driftwood. I made a little pile of my treasures, wondering if Shon or Ray were going to make fun of me for my finds. Surprisingly, they both loved what I'd found. Ray mentioned that he and Riska liked combing the gravel bars for hours looking for unique pieces. I discovered a new hobby. Combing gravel bars was something that I knew that I wanted to do again.

Freeze-Up

We left our PA-12 at Ray's place for Freeze-Up. We were hoping that the lake would freeze quickly and Ray could come out to get Shon in a couple of weeks in his Husky on wheels. Johnny flew us out in his airplane on floats with a big bunch of groceries to hold us over until we could get back to town. The day after we got back, the temperatures plummeted, and we had a half-inch layer of ice form over the surface of our lake. Johnny and Ray both called Shon and congratulated him on timing the float change just right. We were glad to be home, knowing that we would have our airplane back soon. We just needed seven inches of good, clear ice to make a runway on the lake.

Shon and I walked every morning after breakfast. The ground was frozen but free of snow, so we made a little track around the house and did several laps each morning. We enjoyed getting some exercise as we waited for the ice to form. As we made our first trip around our property, we stopped at the lake so that Shon could check the ice. He hit it with a hammer and watched how deep the crack appeared to be. The lake made its eerie noises as the ice grew. Everything was going along nicely until the weather warmed up all of a sudden. We had about two inches when the ice all melted, and we were back to square one. Ray and Johnny both called Shon and told him he messed up on timing the float change. We should have waited another few weeks.

In just a little while, the temperatures made another turn, and the lake started freezing again. This time, we got some frigid weather, resulting in about four inches of ice. We were excited by the progress every morning as we walked by the lake. By this time, Shon was checking the depth of the ice with his chainsaw. At four inches, not only did Shon walk on the lake, he rode his snow machine out on it as I watched nervously from the shore. I'm as brave as they come if I can go second. We were feeling hopeful about getting the plane back soon when we got a massive dump of snow. On Thanksgiving Day, it snowed about thirty inches, covering our good ice with a blanket of fluffy white insulation. That totally messed up our plans. Not only would that much snow require skis instead of wheels, we knew that would halt the forming of the good, clear ice on the lake.

Instead of a restful Thanksgiving, we shoveled snow and Shon packed the runway with his snow machine, hoping to help the ice underneath that deep layer of insulation. It helped some, but he couldn't pack the entire lake. As the days progressed and the temperatures fluctuated, the snow on the lake turned to overflow, a slushy mess. Things were not looking good. We had plenty of snow, but the lake was questionable. It looked like it was going to take a good long time for the runway to form. Shon, Ray, and our neighbor, Roger, all decided we needed to build an airstrip in the muskeg.

Where There is a Will, There is a Way

Shon looked at a satellite view of the surrounding areas. He found a place out in the muskeg that had a clearing about 900-feet long. We rode over to the spot on our snow machines and started to work. Shon showed me where he wanted the runway built, and I placed stakes along the side with big black trash bags attached at the top. Shon used his chainsaw to cut down several small spruce trees that were in the way of our airstrip. I came along after him, moving the trees off of the strip and packing down the snow the best I could with my feet. After we had the area cleared, Roger came over and cut down trees at the east end, allowing for a better approach. Shon and Roger both groomed the strip, over and over, trying to knock down the bumps for a smoother landing. After several days of work, the airstrip was deemed complete.

We notified Ray, and a plan formed for him to fly out to retrieve Shon. We all rode over on our snow machines, watching patiently for the Husky to appear out of the east. We heard him before we saw him. Ray and his bird finally came into view. It was exciting! I hadn't seen anyone except for Shon and Roger in almost two months. He flew over low, getting a good look at our muskeg airstrip, then circled for a landing from the east. As we watched him get into position, he appeared to be coming in too high and fast. He touched down hard, bounced, and throttled back up for a go-around. Once again, I found my heart in my throat. I wondered if my poor soul was going to be able to take all of this. Ray came back around, slower and lower this time, and made a nice landing, although a bumpy one.

When we rode over to the plane, Ray got out, lit a cigarette, and stated that our runway was crap. It was too bumpy. He didn't particularly want to land there again until after we had gotten a little more snow. After a short visit, Shon climbed in for the ride back to town to transition our plane from wheels to skis. There was work to be done. I rode back home, hoping all would go well. As I got closer to home, that dread that I'd fought off in October was back, wrapping itself around my heart, telling me that Shon was sure to crash once again.

In just a few days, the transition from wheels to skis completed and Shon was on his way home. There were about six inches of fresh snow on the new muskeg runway, so I hoped that Shon's landing would be a little smoother than Ray's had been. Roger and I were there to meet him when he came in. Roger videoed Shon's arrival while I held my breath, praying for his safety. Shon circled and chose to land from the west. He came in low and slow, touching the skis down quickly. Red could have been to a full stop halfway down the runway, which made me feel even better about our recently constructed airstrip. He throttled up and taxied the plane toward the East end, causing snow dust to cover Roger and me. When he made it to the end, he did a powered turn, putting the plane in a good position for our next take-off.

Figuring out how to tie the airplane down in the snow was a trick. We thought about it for a while before coming up with a solution. Shon and I dug two holes in the snow, one under each wing. The holes were about twelve inches square and three feet deep. We had two tie downs that we had constructed from twelve-inch square plywood with a rope attached. We placed one in each hole with the rope draping over the side. We shoveled the snow back into the holes over the plywood and stomped it down around the rope. We attached the tie downs to the wings, so the airplane was secure. After we had the PA-12 tied down, we attached the wing covers, tail covers, and engine covers. There were even covers for the propeller and the spinner to help prevent ice from forming on the airplane.

It felt strange leaving the airplane out in the muskeg so far from the house, but we knew she was safe. It wasn't like anyone was going to stumble upon her out in the middle of nowhere. Even though the situation wasn't ideal, we were glad to have her home, and I was looking forward to my first trip to town on skis.

Close Call

I didn't have to wait long for my flight to town. In just a few days, Shon informed me that the weather looked good. I needed to get my grocery list together because we were flying to town. The temperature had peaked at thirty-five degrees Fahrenheit for two days but had come back down to the mid-teens.

Shon took a small generator over to the plane early that morning so he could plug in his engine block and oil sump heater. It needed to run for about three hours for the airplane to be warm enough to fly. After a good breakfast, we loaded up our snow machines and headed back over to the plane. I took the covers off while Shon took care of the generator and untied the ropes. About the time we were climbing in, Ray and Roger landed in the Husky. He was bringing Roger back from a trip to town.

Ray and Roger were unloading the Husky while we were getting ready to take off. Shon throttled up the plane. The tail lifted, but Red wouldn't go anywhere. Shon worked the petals back and forth, trying to break the skis loose, but to no avail. After a few tries, Ray and Roger came over. They each got under a wing and rocked the plane back and forth, breaking the skis away from the snow. The airplane moved forward, and we were off. The take-off took a little longer than what Shon expected, but we were off in plenty of time. I had my eyes closed as we bumped down the runway, but as soon as we took flight, I opened my eyes to see the area break open before me. Once again, I relished the thrill of flight and the beauty of observing the world from above.

We enjoyed the trip to town. The engine was strong, and the view was stunning. I got a little nervous as we neared Ray's airstrip. We flew over Shon's crash site and lined up towards the bluff. Ray's runway was plenty long, but it was narrow and had a slight bend in it. My anxiety shot upward as Shon brought the skis down on the icy strip.

I didn't think the airplane was ever going to stop. We bounced along for an unusually long time. We were still going at a good pace when we went by Ray's hangar on our left. There was still plenty of runway left, but I knew that Shon expected to be turning at that point. There was no way we were going to make the turn. We were going too fast.

I always try to keep my mouth closed during take-offs and landings, but I did ask, "Are we okay?" Shon had just finished reassuring me that things were okay when the plane took a sharp turn to the right. I said nothing, but we were headed straight for the trees. We had turned into deep snow and slowed more quickly than we had before. Before we could even say anything, the airplane stopped.

Shon shut off the plane while I hurried to get my seatbelt off. He'd barely had time to open the door when I jumped out of the airplane. I wanted out of that thing. I looked over the plane and found that the right wing was a mere two inches from one tree. The other wing was only about six inches from another one.

On the one hand, I was thankful that we hadn't crashed. On the other hand, I was *mad*. I couldn't understand why Shon would turn our airplane straight for the trees. I have learned, however, that it doesn't help to raise my voice to my husband. In a very calm, loving voice, I asked him, "Why would you turn us into the trees when we had a perfectly good runway in front of us?"

He looked at me, dumbfounded. "Why would I do that on purpose?"

We waited for Ray. We knew he would be coming in soon and could help pull us out of the snow with his bulldozer. When he landed and saw us with our nose in the trees instead of safely at his hangar, I saw him shake his head. We walked over to him as he got out of the Husky. He grabbed me up and gave me a big hug while asking Shon what had happened. Shon described what the plane did. We walked out to the runway and looked at the tracks made by the skis. Shon and Ray finally saw what had caused the problem. It looked like a clump of ice had stuck on the bottom of the right ski and had acted as a brake when we had slowed down enough. That chunk caught in the snow, making the plane spin around to the right.

In a few hours, we had the airplane out of the deep snow and into Ray's warm hangar. Red was fine. Shon knew that it was a fluke. We just needed to put a piece of wood under our skis when she was parked so they wouldn't freeze to the snow or ice.

I didn't take it quite as well. I had been looking forward to getting into the pilot's seat, but my nerves were shot. Alaska flying was something else. It wasn't anything like the flying I had done in Texas, where I learned to land on a nine-thousand-foot runway that was plenty wide and free of snow. I'd never made an off-airport landing, much less one on a lake or a gravel bar. It felt like *my* dreams of flying were crumbling. There was no way I would ever be able to handle these situations. It was going to take every ounce of courage I could muster to climb back in the plane for the ride home.

Hold It Together

We didn't have to use the muskeg strip for very long. Shon continued to check the lake daily with the chainsaw until the ice was thick enough to land the airplane. After thinking that the lake would never freeze, it finally did. It was finally time to bring Red back to Cub Lake. We had prepared the lake in the same way we had the muskeg, with stakes and big, black trash bags to designate the runway. I took him over on the snow machine one morning. I removed the covers while he dealt with the generator. This time, we had the added step of removing the wood from under the skis. He got in the plane and started her up as I rode back to Cub Lake on the snow machine. I parked up in the yard and waited.

As I sat in the cold, waiting for Shon to land on the lake for the first time, I prayed. God knew the pictures of disasters that were flashing through my mind. I imagined everything that could go wrong. I was so afraid that Shon would crash and I wouldn't know how to help him. I asked God to take away all of the fear that seemed to smother me each time we did something new. I explained to my Heavenly Father that I was terrified of that airplane. I told Him that the PA-12 was fragile. When I'd finished with my prayer, several thoughts came to mind. I didn't need to trust the airplane; I needed to trust God. Instead of God reassuring me that the aircraft was reliable, He pointed out that my body was fragile as well. And He reminded me that in Him, all things hold together. I didn't need to fear; I had to trust.

I heard the airplane as Shon flew around the area a bit. I caught sight of him as he flew over Cub Lake. I knew that Shon was getting into the traffic pattern, preparing to land. He flew over the trees out of sight for a moment, but I could still hear the roar of the engine in the distance. In less than a minute, I saw the plane come through the opening of trees, the airplane low and slow, touching down gently on the snow-covered runway. He slowed down close to the end of the strip, then throttled up, turning to taxi Red to her designated spot on the lawn. Snow dust filled the air, settling a few moments after the engine had come to a complete stop. Shon got out with a big smile on his face.

I decided then and there that I couldn't let fear stop me from my turn in the pilot's seat. I needed to wait a little longer, allowing Shon time to get experience on skis while we both learned about the weather and snow conditions. I was determined to go for it. And if nothing else, the adventure of *me* learning to fly in Alaska could be enough material for my next book.

He is before all things,
and in him all things hold together.

Colossians 1:17 NIV

CHAPTER 12

No Regrets

My adventure didn't begin when we moved to Alaska. It started the night I met Shon at Angelo State University when I made fun of his dirty pants. When I married Shon, I had no idea what a wild ride it would be. His law enforcement career changed us over the years, breaking our trust in people and putting us at odds with each other. The love for our two boys and the commitment we made on our wedding day kept us together. By the time our boys were grown, we were holding on by a thread. Knowing that we needed a drastic change, God sent us on a terrific journey.

Our move to Alaska was not a pretty one. Shon and I made every mistake possible, becoming the talk of the neighborhood we didn't know existed. We questioned our decision to move north quite often those first few months, as did our neighbors, I am sure. I don't know how many times we got stuck, but we eventually figured out how to work together.

Adjusting to life in the wilderness made us appreciate the little things. Living in an area where outhouses are standard and running water isn't has been life-changing. Electricity is a luxury that we don't take for granted. Buying only what we need has become a way of life. Many people move to the wilderness to be self-sufficient, to be less dependent on society. I get that. In some ways, we have become more reliant on ourselves, but in other ways, we are more dependent than ever before. We always need help from our friends in town. We find ourselves thankful for essential goods and services. Invariably, something breaks, and we need a new part. By living off-grid, away from society, we have developed a deeper appreciation for people and how much we all need each other.

Not only have we developed a greater respect for people, but we have also grown in our respect for the weather. One of our favorite aspects of Alaska is the four distinct seasons. They remind us that life changes quickly. We need to appreciate the current season that we are experiencing. Longing for days gone by or wishing for days ahead is futile. We have learned to find a purpose for the day at hand, even if it is not perfect. We have also realized that what is possible in one season can be impossible in another season. We can walk across the frozen river in the winter, but wouldn't dare attempt it in the summer. If there is something we want to do, but it seems impossible, we might need to wait until the time is right. That was not a concept that we fully grasped in Texas.

The flying in Alaska has been magnificent, but any flight can change quickly. Flying has always been deeply spiritual for me. Lifting off of the ground and getting an aerial view of life below has reminded me of God's perspective. I'm more aware of God's view of me and my surroundings. He has a much better view from above than I have from the ground. I'm also distinctly aware of staying out of the clouds and keeping an eye on the weather. That's no different than reading the Bible to keep my eyes open to the truth, so I don't get lost in the "soup." It is pretty simple, but flying reminds me to stay connected to the one who sees all and to trust His directions.

Shon and I went from being stuck in the mud at every turn to lifting off and flying over that dreadful muskeg. What a perfect picture of how our relationship progressed during our time here! Instead of each having separate jobs, Shon and I finally had a common focus. We couldn't retreat to our own worlds when we disagreed. There was nowhere else to go. And there were jobs that we had to do that required both of us. Some of the tasks, like processing a tree, Shon could do alone, but we quickly realized that it went more than twice as fast when I helped. And we slowly started having a greater appreciation for each other's strengths. A chore that could be draining for one became an event that we looked forward to doing as a team. Slowly but surely, that mindset has bled over to other aspects of our life as well, making our time together much sweeter. We still get stuck from time to time, but we are much better at getting out of the mess quickly and without much drama. Yes, we went from being stuck in the muck to flying high in the sky.

And then there was the crash. That horrible day, November 1, will forever be burned into my brain. It was hard, but we didn't question God's goodness or His love for us. It didn't make us fearful of death. It reminded us of the promise of heaven when we leave this life. I don't particularly want to die a horrible death, crashing through the trees and then burning alive, but I know where I get to spend eternity. And it isn't determined by my goodness, but by God's grace and the sacrifice made by Jesus. It is a gift that I readily accepted when I figured out I didn't have all of the answers, but God did. The crash could have kept us from living a full life, but through the confidence we have in Christ, we don't have to fear. That's not to say that I don't deal with fear. I fight it daily, and I know I'm not alone.

We arrived at the cabin on Cub Lake with broken hearts. A couple of years later, we had even more injuries that required our attention. It took time, but God healed the physical and the emotional. Shon has a deep scar along the left side of his face. There are other scars that no one can see, but God used this wild, rugged place to heal us. He brought us together, He drew us closer to Him, and He gave us the adventure of a lifetime. What blessings we would have missed if we would have succumbed to the fear and hadn't followed God when He whispered in His still, small voice, "Follow Me to Alaska."

Can two walk together,
except they be agreed?

Amos 3:3 KJV

For more stories, pictures, and videos,
go to *www.followmetoalaska.com* or
check out our Facebook page, Follow Me to Alaska.

About the Author

Ann Parker was born in Las Cruces, New Mexico. Her younger years were spent in Carrizozo, New Mexico, trying to keep up with her two older siblings, Carrie and Wayland. They told her she could only tag along "if she could keep up." Her fear of being left out created a strong determination in her formative years. That drive equipped her to keep pace with her siblings, who were six and seven years her senior. She also spent time bossing around her younger brother, Patrick. Her mother remembers Ann, just a kindergartener, instructing two-year-old Patrick to recite the pledge of allegiance. Patrick definitely had a hand in developing Ann's love for teaching.

Ann's family moved to a small West Texas town, Sonora, when she was just ten years old. Sonora proved to be a nurturing, idyllic place to grow up. Ann enjoyed being involved in as many activities as time would allow. She especially loved the competition of basketball and track, while forging friendships with teammates that have lasted throughout the years. The people of Sonora helped develop her faith and convictions that have shaped her life.

Her education continued at Angelo State University, where she earned a Bachelor of Science in Education. During her time at the university, she met Shon at Casino Night. After a brief courtship, they married while she was still in school, and he was beginning his career in law enforcement.

Ann taught third grade for two years at Water Valley Elementary before Kyle was born. At that time, she and Shon decided Ann needed to be a stay-at-home mom. Three years later, the family grew with the arrival of Jared. After nine years, Shon left the San Angelo Police Department to work for the Texas Department of Public Safety. This change led the family to move to Big Spring, Texas, which was close to Shon's hometown of Ackerly.

Over the years, Ann went back to teaching elementary and eventually taught high school-level mathematics. Shon and Ann both got their pilot licenses, which created a new opportunity for Shon's career. They lived in Alpine, Texas, for a few years, followed by a time in El Paso. After twenty-eight years in law enforcement, Shon retired, and the couple made the most daring move of their life.

Ann's writing developed through the telling of many Alaskan adventures and misadventures on Facebook. Her friends and family loved the stories, asking her to continue writing about life in the land of the Last Frontier. Because of their solitude, Ann especially enjoyed the interaction from her friends, even if only online. Throughout this process, an unsuspecting author and this book were born.

Printed in Great Britain
by Amazon

32935880R00145